Cambridge Elements

Elements in Histories of Emotions and the Senses
edited by
Jan Plamper
Goldsmiths, University of London

THE EVOLUTION OF AFFECT THEORY

The Humanities, the Sciences, and the Study of Power

Donovan O. Schaefer
University of Pennsylvania

CAMBRIDGE
UNIVERSITY PRESS

CAMBRIDGE
UNIVERSITY PRESS

University Printing House, Cambridge CB2 8BS, United Kingdom

One Liberty Plaza, 20th Floor, New York, NY 10006, USA

477 Williamstown Road, Port Melbourne, VIC 3207, Australia

314–321, 3rd Floor, Plot 3, Splendor Forum, Jasola District Centre,
New Delhi – 110025, India

79 Anson Road, #06–04/06, Singapore 079906

Cambridge University Press is part of the University of Cambridge.

It furthers the University's mission by disseminating knowledge in the pursuit of education, learning, and research at the highest international levels of excellence.

www.cambridge.org
Information on this title: www.cambridge.org/9781108732116
DOI: 10.1017/9781108765343

First published 2019

A catalogue record for this publication is available from the British Library.

ISBN 978-1-108-73211-6 (paperback)
ISSN 2632-1068 (online)
ISSN 2632-105X (print)

Cambridge University Press has no responsibility for the persistence or accuracy of URLs for external or third-party internet websites referred to in this publication and does not guarantee that any content on such websites is, or will remain, accurate or appropriate.

The Evolution of Affect Theory

The Humanities, the Sciences, and the Study of Power

Elements in Histories of Emotions and the Senses

DOI: 10.1017/9781108765343
First published online: May 2019

Donovan O. Schaefer
University of Pennsylvania

Author for correspondence: Donovan O. Schaefer, doschaef@sas.upenn.edu

Abstract: Across the humanities, a set of interrelated concepts – excess, becoming, the event – have gained purchase as analytical tools for thinking about power. Some versions of affect theory rely on Gilles Deleuze's concept of "becoming," proposing that affect is best understood as a field of dynamic novelty. Reconsidering affect theory's relationship with life sciences, Schaefer argues that this procedure fails as a register of the analytics of power. By way of a case study, this Element concludes with a return to the work of Saba Mahmood, in particular her 2005 study of the women's mosque movement in Cairo, *Politics of Piety.*

Keywords: affect, evolution, power, Saba Mahmood, Gilles Deleuze

ISBNs: 9781108732116 (PB), 9781108765343 (OC)
ISSNs: 2632-1068 (online), 2632-105X (print)

Contents

Introduction: Music without Words   1

1 The Deleuzian Dialect of Affect Theory   6

2 Unbecoming: Criticisms of the Deleuzian Dialect of Affect Theory   22

3 The Animality of Affect   33

4 Economies of Dignity: Reconsidering the Mosque Movement   53

Conclusion: The Entertainment   61

Bibliography   67

Acknowledgments   73

Introduction: Music without Words

"Why do we love music that is without words?" –
Hélène Cixous and Mireille Calle-Gruber, *Rootprints*

The journalist Chuck Todd, host of the American political talk show "Meet the Press," was asked, shortly after the successful presidential campaign of Donald J. Trump in 2016, to reflect on what he saw as the most distinctive features of the president-elect. He said that Trump has a peculiar habit after he finishes taping an interview: he sits in the studio and asks to watch the playback, with the sound off. Todd proposed that Trump's effectiveness as a politician needs to be understood in part through his acute sensitivity to the visual aspects of his performance (Thrush 2016). What is this political efficacy that flows, not from language, but from a face? How can a face, a body, an image, a place, or an object conduct power? Kathleen Stewart writes that "power is a thing of the senses" (Stewart 2007, 84). How do the felt or sensed dimensions of power – not just surrounding individual leaders, but throughout the field of politics – fuel the vast machines making and unmaking societies?

Affect theory is an approach to history, politics, culture, and all other aspects of embodied life that emphasizes the role of nonlinguistic and non- or para-cognitive forces. As a method, affect theory asks *what bodies do* – what they want, where they go, what they think, how they decide – and especially how bodies are impelled by forces other than language and reason. It is, therefore, also a theory of power. For affect theory, feelings, emotions, affects, moods, and sensations are not cosmetic but rather the substance of subjectivity. Unlike liberal approaches that see emotion as the antithesis of political reason, however, affect theory is designed to explain progressive, democratic, and even liberal movements themselves just as well as it explains the appeal of conservatism, reaction, and fascism.

This Element is about the relationship of bodies to affects and, in particular, the conceptual ambidexterity of the term *affect* itself. Affect theory, as scholars such as Sara Ahmed, Eugenie Brinkema, Mel Y. Chen, Ann Cvetkovich, Eve Sedgwick, Greg Seigworth, and Melissa Gregg have pointed out, tracks into divergent, and perhaps incommensurable, definitions: *affect*, in a sense used by thinkers inspired by Gilles Deleuze, as something like unstructured proto-sensation, and *affects*, in a sense used by theorists drawing on blends of feminism, queer theory, emotion psychology, and phenomenology as the felt emotional textures structuring our embodied experience.[1] In the former, *affect* is

---

[1] See Ahmed 2004c; Brinkema 2014; Chen 2012; Cvetkovich 2012; Gregg and Seigworth 2010; Sedgwick 2003.

often aligned with a chain of rhyming concepts inherited from French philosophy that have currency across the humanities, such as *becoming, intensity, excess, the event,* and *the virtual.* This sense of affect is rigidly separated from the realm of "conscious" emotions. In the latter, a more casual approach allows an easy interchangeability of *affect* with terms such as *emotion* and *feeling* and a cross-cutting of registers from the "conscious" to the "unconscious." Both of these definitions are off to the side of a common definitional practice in the psychology of emotions, which pitches *affect* as a micro-register of feeling and *emotion* as a macro-register. I'll return to discuss this use in the final section of this Element.

My argument here is focused on the landscape of this debate and makes a specific intervention: I argue that a theory of affect *and power* can't work if affect is defined as *becoming.* I propose that we need the second version of affect theory in order to understand the relationship between affect and formations of power. The Deleuzian understanding of affect is not irrelevant to accounts of power. But it ultimately indexes something so far upstream of bodies that it is oblivious to the way that power interfaces with organisms in their animal specificity. I follow scholars such as Ann Cvetkovich and Sara Ahmed, then, in preferring that the concept of *affect* remains entangled with terms such as *feeling* and *emotion* rather than rigidly chambered in a nonlinguistic, noncognitive, nonpersonal field.

In the course of developing this argument, this Element engages in a sustained way with the relationship between affect theory and the life sciences. Affect theory's encounter with the sciences is driven, in part, by an attempt to reframe the way the humanities are done. But what understanding of the life sciences leads this discussion? What is the "evolution" of affect theory? I argue that the evolutionary approach conducts us to special attention to the animality of bodies – what Elizabeth A. Wilson has called their *bio-logic* – as a major touchstone for thinking about the domain of affect. Affects in their *animality* need to be understood in terms of concrete dynamics between change and structure, becoming and being, rather than governed by an overarching logic of becoming. I argue that this approach clarifies how affect theory attaches to what Michel Foucault calls the "analytics of power."

The analytics of power focuses on exactly this kind of detailed mapping. The insistence on detail comes across already in Foucault's suggestion that an *analytics of power* is distinguished from a *theory of power* by virtue of tracking the concrete mechanisms by which power is distributed. Crucially for Foucault, this distribution system must be distinguished from a top-down understanding in which power is implemented from above, what he calls the *juridico-discursive model* of power. The analytics of power proposes, by contrast, that power is always (with the exception of limit cases) *productive* as well as constraining.

Power would not work, Foucault suggests, if it were only an endlessly repeated *no* backed up by force. Instead, we must turn to a conception of power that creates situations that bodies want. He writes that the analytics of power is

> a conception of power which replaces the privilege of the law with the viewpoint of the objective, the privilege of prohibition with the viewpoint of tactical efficacy, the privilege of sovereignty with the analysis of a multiple and mobile field of force relations, wherein far-reaching, but never completely stable, effects of domination are produced. (Foucault 1990, 102)

Multiplicity, force relations, and a dynamic of variability and stability are the hallmarks of Foucault's understanding of power.

Although Foucault refused to ask after the nature of power itself – preferring to focus on "the little question, *What happens?*" rather than the grand question, *What is it?* (Foucault 1982, 217, emphasis added) – affect theory would seem to offer resources for deepening our understanding of the nature of power (see Schaefer 2015, chapter 1). Foucault seems to want to move the analytics of power out of the domain of a rationalist paradigm preoccupied with centralization: "let us not look for the headquarters that presides over its rationality," he proposes, before continuing, "the logic is perfectly clear, the aims decipherable, and yet it is often the case that no one is there to have invented them, and few who can be said to have formulated them: an implicit characteristic of the great anonymous, almost unspoken strategies which coordinate the loquacious tactics whose 'inventors' or decisionmakers are often without hypocrisy" (Foucault 1990, 95). This is an entry point for plugging in a theory of affect, which is similarly interested in conceptualizing power's fuzzy relationship with intention, cognition, accident, awareness, and what gets called "reason."

Hélène Cixous asks the deceptively simple question, "Why do we love music that is without words?" (Cixous & Calle-Gruber 1997, 46). Why *do* we love music without words? What is the force – riding airborne vibrations – reverberating deep into our bodies that makes us move? What other unspoken forces shape our embodied subjectivity? Where Foucault proposed a model of *power-knowledge*, affect theory suggests that we need to think of *power-affect* – or *power-knowledge-affect*. But here we're returned to the question of the relationship between affect and "consciousness." The argument advanced here will propose that the evanescent sense of affect as *becoming*, or *excess*, or *the event* – radically exterior to the field of "the personal" – is too slippery to capture the traction of power. It simply doesn't exist in the realm of the contestable, the material, the concrete – the realm where forces crash against each other and crumple or prevail.

To set up the story of affect theory as it tracks different lines of intellectual development, the section "The Deleuzian Dialect of Affect Theory" explores the trajectory of affect theory along the Deleuzian stream. It studies the dynamic of *affections* and *affects* in Spinoza and how these categories yield Spinoza's complex understanding of embodiment and animality. It then cuts forward to Deleuze's early work on Spinoza and Bergson, revealing how Deleuze's alternating fascinations with Spinoza and Bergson build up a pronounced tension within his work. This is particularly salient in Deleuze's own theory of animals, offered in his later work with Félix Guattari. Where Deleuze is most strongly tinged by Bergson, he tends to take *affect* to be something that is essentially prior to *the personal*. Along these lines, commentators such as Brian Massumi promote a version of affect that is fundamentally exterior to cognition, language, and emotion. *Affect* becomes a capsule or convergence point for a set of isomorphic themes that all reiterate this essential exteriority – *becoming, excess, virtuality, novelty*, and *the event*.

Criticisms of this dialect of affect theory are examined in the section "Unbecoming" with an eye to highlighting the limitations of a definition of affect as synonymous with becoming (and so essentially external to capture). A review of contemporary evolutionary biology's attention to the necessary dynamic *between* structure and change demonstrates that Massumi's theory of animality – which exclusively stresses becoming – misses crucial elements needed for an account of embodied life. This dynamic presentation can be found in a reading of some strands of Deleuze's own thought, primarily those that have the most distance from Bergson. This line of criticism partially overlaps with the challenge to affect theory put forward by scholars such as Ruth Leys.

The section "The Animality of Affect" advances a new framing of affect theory as a way of analyzing power. It suggests that affect provides an excellent lens for thinking of humans as existing in continuity with nonhuman animals, as Darwin himself foresaw in *The Expression of the Emotions in Man and Animals*. By centralizing the nonlinguistic elements of subjectivity, it exposes the implicit assumption, present throughout the humanities, that subjectivity requires language. This highlights the way that the line from humans to animals is not a passage from subjectivity to nonsubjectivity but through a range of embodied forms of subjectivity.

This prompts consideration of a second lineage of affect theory – that which is primarily advocated by queer and feminist scholars of affect such as Eve Sedgwick and Sara Ahmed. This lineage has dialects of its own. One of these is

Sedgwick's queer reframing of psychologist Silvan Tomkins, who built a version of affect theory drawing on Darwin. Tomkins uses affect in a sense more closely attached to psychoanalysis but elaborates a sophisticated framework that detaches the concept of affect from Freud's concept of drives and makes it central to a new theory of motivation. Sedgwick revisits and modifies this framework, devising an understanding of affect that is comfortable with a more intimate set of links between affect, emotion, and cognition. A related dialect is the phenomenological tradition championed by Sara Ahmed, which emphasizes the constitution of the subject through a play of recursive impressions that shape the horizon of feeling.

I show that these lines of thought can be brought together to highlight the limitations of theories of affect that emphasize *becoming*. The risk of locating affect in the register of becoming is shown to be not only an insufficient attention to the material conditions of evolved embodiment but also an insufficient account of the operations of power, which, as Foucault has shown, necessarily play out in an inescapable dynamic of opening *and* constraint. Foucault's analytics of power, it is proposed, are productively supplemented by an attention to a broader sense of affect. In particular, much as an account of evolution, contra Massumi, needs to include attention to both repetition and change, so an account of power needs to expand beyond the channel of *becoming*. Criticisms of Tomkins' Basic Emotions hypothesis and his anti-intentionalism are also considered here.

The closing section, "Economies of Dignity: Reconsidering the Mosque Movement," applies the revised understanding of affect in its animality to Saba Mahmood's account of a women's mosque movement in Egypt during her fieldwork in the 1990s. The mosque movement brought together a number of female Muslim leaders who opted, within the context of a putatively secular society, to reintroduce elements of Islamic piety, such as the cultivation of modesty and the wearing of the hijab. Mahmood sees the mosque movement women as suggesting ways to push beyond liberal/secular narratives that insist on a necessary movement away from religion and toward autonomy. Rather, she suggests, her consultants indicate the diversity and variety of forms of agency in the world – not all of which can be subordinated to a binary of free/unfree.

My revisiting of Mahmood's work takes a different framing, drawing in part on Mahmood's own work on affect in later pieces such as "Religious Reason and Secular Affect" (Mahmood 2007). I argue that the affect theory approach to the mosque movement helps us to think beyond the category of *agency* itself. This version of affect, however, cannot be a synonym for *becoming*, which misses what is happening with the mosque movement entirely. Instead, the mapping of the dynamic between religion, bodies, and power requires a more textured account of the play of emotion and repetition. Integrating writings on shame from Tomkins and Sedgwick with Sara Ahmed's notion of the *affective economy*, I propose that the mosque movement can be understood against the backdrop of a broader *economy of dignity*. This backdrop provides the coordinates of power within which religious subjects make decisions and navigate their material-affective situations.

Affect theory is at a stage where it will benefit from a survey of its concepts and a clearer delineation of its analytical tool kit. This Element is not designed to resolve this discussion, but it is designed to advance it. It seeks to do so by examining affect theory as a unique zone of engagement between the humanities and the sciences and addressing the primary criticisms that have been levied against it. All told, the understanding of affect in the light of evolution – thinking of affect, in other words, as animal – provides a comprehensive template for thinking about how power interfaces with bodies, whether in secular or religious contexts. Slitting the binary between "conscious" and "preconscious" creates a more versatile theory of power, while also shining a light on how the humanities and the sciences can strengthen the dialogue between them.

1 The Deleuzian Dialect of Affect Theory

The setting was the Center for 21st Century Studies (C21), a research unit at the University of Wisconsin–Milwaukee. It was their 2012 conference, on the theme "The Non-human Turn." On the ground floor of the concrete tower that housed C21, philosopher-artists Erin Manning and Brian Massumi had set up an installation piece, "Weather Patterns." Sited next to the registration area outside the main lecture room, the installation was a mass of black fabric and cables suspended from the ceiling. Conference-goers passed through it like a maze of curtains on their way to the theater (an image of the piece has been posted here: www.flickr.com/photos/nathanielstern/7302487294/in/photostream/).

There were also speakers embedded in the folds of the cloth. The cloth wasn't ordinary fabric. It had been wired up to act as an antenna. The fabric was picking up waves of air from the motion of passersby and absorbing the waves as electronic signals. The signals were collated and converted into sound, which was then emitted by the speakers. The subtle, unpredictable, cross-cutting air currents were transformed into noise. The effect was a cascade of whispering, screeching, and clicking emanating from the cloth and rolling through the concrete halls.

The artwork modeled Massumi and Manning's understanding of affect: a field of pure potential that circulates between bodies. This version of affect is itself built on the understanding of affect offered by Benedict de Spinoza, as the play of the "infinitely many things in infinitely many modes" (Spinoza 1996, 13), the unfurling of a single substance, what Gilles Deleuze would later call the "plane of immanence" (Deleuze 1988b, 122). As Massumi and Manning wrote of the piece, it was the materialization of "[a] process" that would "[r]egister the environmental conditions in a series of relational cross-currents" (C21 2012, np). The art-machine took this idea of affect – as abstract micro-processes crashing between bodies – and rendered it audible.

Walking through Weather Patterns on the way to sessions was fun – you never knew quite what it was going to do. After a few encounters, however, I came to the conclusion that it was better appreciated at a distance. It was still fascinating. On the last day of the conference, I left the final session a few minutes early. The registration table still had a grad student working at it. She was about twenty feet from Weather Patterns, which was still clicking and whispering away. I realized that she had been effectively sitting *inside the installation* for hours. She was staring straight ahead with her arms folded. I walked up to her and asked, "So has this lost its charm for you?" Still staring straight ahead, arms folded, without looking up, she responded, "I need a drink."

Ann Cvetkovich's *Depression: A Public Feeling* opens with an important preface for any discussion of what now gets called *affect theory*. Although the term itself is relatively new, she notes, attention to affect has been a part of certain scholarly disciplines – including, especially, feminism, queer theory, anti-racism, and postcolonial studies – decades before anyone came up with the phrase "the affective turn" (Cvetkovich 2012, 3ff; see also Wiegman 2014, 13). But within the contemporary discussion, Cvetkovich notes two subtly distinct methodological flavors. In one stream is the loose network of scholars, such as the Public Feelings Collective, who thematize affect as the matrix of feeling at the personal level. In the other stream are what Cvetkovich calls the *Deleuzians*, affect theorists who define affect in a technical sense devised by the philosopher Gilles Deleuze. In Cvetkovich's account, the distinction between these branches lies in the decision to use a technical or blurred definition of affect: Deleuzians tend to rigidly maintain the border between something called *affect* – that is, "precognitive sensory experience and relations to surroundings" – and something called *emotion* – "cultural constructs and conscious processes that emerge from them, such as anger, fear, or joy" (Cvetkovich 2012, 4). Cvetkovich herself professes the first branch, deploying a less disciplined use of the term *affect* as "encompass[ing] affect, emotion, and feeling, and that includes impulses, desires, and feelings that get historically constructed in a range of ways" (Cvetkovich 2012, 4). Sara Ahmed calls this second perspective – less committed to the differentiation between affect and emotion – "feminist cultural studies of affect" (Ahmed 2010, 13).

The Deleuzian approach to affect has been advanced primarily in the fields of poststructuralist philosophy and media studies. Massumi, one of its most prominent exponents, has provided a brilliant exposition of Deleuze's notion of affect, featured in Deleuze's early works on Spinoza and Bergson and in his later collaborations with Félix Guattari, some of which Massumi himself translated for Anglophone audiences. In this section, I will survey the emergence of the Deleuzian branch of affect theory, paying particular attention to its consideration of animality as a clue to how it interfaces with the biological. I want to study the way in which Deleuze brings together different philosophical ancestor figures – such as Baruch Spinoza and Henri Bergson – into a single philosophical elixir. My suggestion is that there's a tension between these figures as thinkers of affect. When Deleuze's thought is synthesized into a dialect of *affect theory* by Massumi and others, it carries this tension forward, leaving a set of unresolved philosophical problems – and possibly missteps – on the table. This survey will set the stage for a more sustained engagement with criticisms of the Deleuzian dialect in the section "Unbecoming: Criticisms of the Deleuzian Dialect of Affect Theory."

Spinoza, Affections, and Affects

The road to the Deleuzian dialect of affect theory begins with Spinoza, though the exact vocabulary used changes forms many times. In the opening section of Spinoza's *Ethics,* entitled "Of God," he premises his discussion of affects on a discussion of the classical medieval problem of substance and accident, looped through an explicitly theological agenda. Spinoza's theology is monism: God is coextensive with all that is – substance. God, for Spinoza, is "a substance consisting of infinite attributes, each of which expresses eternal and infinite essence" (Spinoza 1996, 7). Spinoza identifies these attributes of substance as what he calls *affections* (Spinoza 1996, 1). "A substance," he proposes, "is prior in nature to its affections" (Spinoza 1996, 2). Affections, then, are the ensemble of properties attached to the universal divinity field of substance.

This monist view of substance is woven, in the second part of *Ethics*, into Spinoza's theory of the relationship between mind and body. Once again, the emphasis is on collapsing dualist accounts of mind and body (Spinoza 1996, 68). In contrast to Descartes, Spinoza asserts, on the basis of the singularity of divine substance, "that the human mind is united to the body" (Spinoza 1996, 40). Spinoza rejects those philosophical understandings of mind that place its operations outside of the "common laws of Nature" (Spinoza 1996, 68–9).

Perception, for Spinoza, is not a transcendent faculty observing the body's affections but rather a sort of *bouncing of affections off of one another within the body* (Spinoza 1996, 50). In the consummate statement of the monist worldview, Spinoza insists that "[i]f things have nothing in common with one another, one of them cannot be the cause of the other" (Spinoza 1996, 3). A perceiving stuff has to be, in an essential sense, *like* the stuff it perceives.

So far, we get a sense of Spinoza as a metaphysician, a thinker cutting against the grain of the great dualist philosophical-theological schemes. But in the third part of *Ethics*, we get Spinoza the psychologist, integrating his version of philosophical monism with an account of how human beings work. He now begins writing about *affects* (not affections) in a seemingly different register. "By affect," Spinoza writes, "I understand affections of the body by which the body's power of acting is increased or diminished, aided or restrained" (Spinoza 1996, 70). The core formation of affect, for Spinoza, is the polarity of *joy* and *sadness* (Spinoza 1996, 77). From this basic continuum, Spinoza spools off a series of meditations on the affects, not only joy and sadness in sections II and III, but wonder (IV), hate (VII), devotion (X), hope (XII), confidence (XIV), despair (XV), gladness (XVI), indignation (XX), compassion (XXIV), repentance (XXVII), pride (XXVIII), despondency (XXIX), shame (XXXI), thankfulness (XXXIV), cruelty (XXXVIII), and ambition (XLIV).

These affects are related to the metaphysical picture of the play of substance-affection to the extent that they follow from Spinoza's monist ontology. But they are also a meaningful departure. Spinoza's characterization of the effects – on groups and individuals – of the different patterns of *affect* has no necessary relationship to his metaphysical monism. We are not in a realm where any particular metaphysical commitments are necessary. The fact that the same genre – a catalogue of emotion words and their meaning – is replicated in Descartes' own late work *The Passions of the Soul* would seem to speak to this.[2]

It's also in this context that Spinoza outlines a theory of animals. Consistent with his monist metaphysics, he refuses to locate animals and humans on opposite sides of a binary division, as Descartes did: "after we know the origin of the mind," he argues, "we cannot in any way doubt that the lower animals feel things" (Spinoza 1996, 101–2). But he also begins a sketch of a way of exploring animal psychology, proposing that humans and different animals *feel differently*. "Both the horse and the man are driven by a lust to procreate," he observes, "but the one is driven by an equine lust, the other by a human lust" (Spinoza 1996, 102). Spinoza's theory of animality is a way of recognizing the

---

[2] That said, the first thing to say about this work is that its metaphysics are complicated and may even reflect a break or evolution from Descartes' earlier works. See Sullivan (2018) for discussion.

embodied particularity of each animal, different organisms – structured biological entities – corresponding to different formations of desire, happiness, and,
one assumes, distinct (but by no means unrelated) suites of affects.

Deleuze's Spinoza, Deleuze's Bergson

Deleuze engages with Spinoza continually throughout his career, including
a pair of books, written two years apart in the late 1960s, *Expressionism in
Philosophy: Spinoza* and *Spinoza: Practical Philosophy*. Like Spinoza, he
stresses the consubstantiality of body and mind: "what is an action in
the mind is necessarily an action in the body as well, and what is a passion in
the body is necessarily a passion in the mind. There is no primacy of one series
over the other" (Deleuze 1988b, 18). And like Spinoza, he emphasizes the
polarity of *joy* and *sadness* as the spectrum on which we respond to that
which enables or dissipates flourishing (Deleuze 1988b, 50).

Deleuze even builds an ad hoc theory of animality along lines similar to
Spinoza's, which he glosses as a project of *ethology*, or description of
animal characteristics. At the end of *Practical Philosophy*, he stresses that to
be animal is fundamentally to be a sum of affections: "given an animal, what is
this animal unaffected by in the infinite world? What does it react to positively
or negatively? What are its nutriments and its poisons? What does it 'take' in its
world?" (Deleuze 1988b, 125). Deleuze even syncs Spinoza up with the founder
of ethology, Jakob von Uexküll (whom we'll revisit in the section "The
Animality of Affect"), proposing that von Uexküll's attention to the "beacons"
of the lifeworld is really a map of an organism's affects (Deleuze 1988b, 124).
To be an animal, whether human or otherwise, is to be defined by the ensemble
of ways that one is affectionately wrapped up with the world.

But at the same time, Deleuze begins to put his own backspin on Spinoza's
ontological tableau. You could call it a sort of romanticism – a Nietzschefication
of Spinoza that plays up the noble, existential tones of his philosophy – especially as revealed in the prismatic light of Spinoza's biography. For instance,
Deleuze makes a sort of proclamatory statement about joy and sadness passing
beyond good and evil: "the good or strong individual is the one who exists so
fully or so intensely that he has gained eternity in his lifetime, so that death,
always extensive, always external, is of little significance to him" (Deleuze
1988b, 41). This is not exactly wrong, vis-à-vis Spinoza, but it's definitely more
Prussia than Amsterdam. Even Spinoza's political situation, as a freethinker,
blasphemer, and religious outcast, is made into a philosophical touchstone, an
endorsement of liberalism according to the coordinates of a kind of vitalist
existentialism: "The best society, then, will be one that exempts the power of

thinking from the obligation to obey, and takes care, in its own interest, not to subject thought to the rule of the state, which only applies to actions. As long as thought is free, hence vital, nothing is compromised" (Deleuze 1988b, 4).

This romantic touching-up of Spinoza eventually merges with another philosophical priority explored by Deleuze: the rediscovery of "true differences in kind or articulations of the real" as they are articulated in the work of Henri Bergson (Deleuze 1988a, 21). Deleuze's *Bergsonism*, from the same period as the Spinoza books, reflects this tension. Deleuze becomes fascinated by Bergson's series of what he calls *differences in kind: duration-space, quality-quantity, heterogeneous-homogeneous, continuous-discontinuous, memory-matter, recollection-perception, contraction-relaxation, instinct-intelligence*. For Bergson, the line of subjectivity – which features affectivity, recollection memory, and contraction memory – *differs in kind* from the line of perception-object-matter (Deleuze 1988a, 25–6). Deleuze hastens to add that this is not a bona fide dualism, but only a provisional dualism that eventually sees a reconciliation of the lines of divergence at a "virtual point" beyond the turn (Deleuze 1988a, 29). We could call it a sort of *spectral dualism* – a dualism that eventually resolves, but nonetheless provides a conceptual scaffolding that encourages the distribution of philosophical concepts into discrete chambers.

The interval within the brain between intelligence and the instinctive responses installed by society is, in Deleuze's interpretation, filled by *emotion*. Emotion "differs in nature from both intelligence and instinct, from both intelligent individual egoism and quasi-instinctive social pressure" (Deleuze 1988a, 110a). But as Deleuze explains in a footnote, what Bergson means by *creative emotion* is really a way of naming *affectivity* (Deleuze 1988a, 134, en 34). Deleuze's concern, then, is with a sort of purified, stripped-down *emotion* in Bergson's sense – emotion as "potential, the nature of emotion as pure element" (Deleuze 1988a, 110). In other words, he's drawing Bergson's vocabulary and Spinoza's into a new blend. "Emotion" becomes that which "precedes all representation, itself generating new ideas" (Deleuze 1988a, 110).

This emotion is stripped from the possibility of having an object. It is, Bergson writes, like "a piece of music which expresses love. It is not love for a particular person . . . . The quality of love will depend upon its essence and not upon its object" (in Deleuze 1988a, 110). Rather than music introducing feelings in us, Bergson proposes, music "introduces us rather into them" (in Deleuze 1988a, 110). Bergson's realm of emotion preexists us – preexists all objects – and instead subsists as a realm of pure potential. "Although personal," Deleuze suggests, "it is not individual; transcendent, it is like the God in us" (Deleuze 1988a, 110). We see again Deleuze's soaring romanticism: "creative emotion" is named as that which "liberates man from the plane or the level that is proper to him, in order to make him a creator" – an alchemical transformation that "undoubtedly only takes place in privileged souls" (Deleuze 1988a, 111).

But in this same romantic swelling, there seems to be a sharp pivot away from the emphasis on the concrete multiplicity of animal bodies we found in Deleuze's reading of Spinoza. Deleuze quotes Bergson as proposing that the task of pursuing "experience at its source" leads us "above that decisive *turn*, where, taking a bias in the direction of our utility, it becomes properly *human* experience" (in Deleuze 1988a, 27). The mystical locus of Bergson's thought that has so entranced Deleuze leads back to a sort of anthropocentrism in which humans are not one animal among many, but a being with a special destiny to harness the plane of "creative emotion."

This compounding of Bergson and Spinoza continues in Deleuze's subsequent work. *A Thousand Plateaus*, his collaboration with Félix Guattari in 1980, sees these digressing intellectual tendencies welded together within a single volume. In the introductory chapter, "The Rhizome," Deleuze and Guattari lay out a picture of radical interconnectedness – a deep ontological continuity that potentially links anything to any other thing. The rhizome – a botanical term referring to underground stems that can shoot out rootlike structures from nodes, each of which may have the potential to generate a new plant – is their controlling image, an entity that "assumes very diverse forms, from ramified surface extension in all directions to concretion into bulbs and tubers" (Deleuze & Guattari 1987, 7).

This radical interconnectedness is a reiteration of the fundamentally Spinozist theme of the unity of substance. All multiplicities can be seen as interlinked to make up a single plane of substance. A break in the rhizome only produces more links, more rhizomes, an ever-expanding network of multiplicities (Deleuze & Guattari 1987, 9). The rhizome is, then, intolerant of duality: the effort to trace a dualism in which something escapes the rhizome – a line of flight – is, in fact, fully sutured to the rhizome (Deleuze & Guattari 1987, 9). Although Deleuze and Guattari dismiss God as the master signifier who wants to obliterate all zones of intensity – Bodies without Organs – they have replicated the conceptual blueprint of Spinoza's God as the unity of all modes of substance, all that is and can ever be.

This ontological picture is overlaid with a roadmap for the production of what Deleuze and Guattari call *intensities*. They light up this path, in part, by attacking classical psychoanalysis, which they accuse of taking the rhizomatic structure of memory and experience and "arborifying" it. Like Procrustes, psychoanalysis blocks the intensities of creativity by carving a sprawling expanse of thought until it fits a strictly vertical mold. But, Deleuze and Guattari insist, "[n]othing is beautiful or loving or political aside from underground stems and aerial roots, adventitious growths and rhizomes" (Deleuze & Guattari 1987, 15). This anti-psychoanalytic critique becomes the idiom for a channel of romantic-existential urgency running through the book: "Don't bring out the General in you!," they cry. "Don't have just ideas, just have an idea (Godard). Have short-term ideas. Make maps, not photos or drawings. Be the Pink Panther and your loves will be like the wasp and the orchid, the cat and the baboon" (Deleuze & Guattari 1987, 25). These early exhortations set the tone for Plateau 6, "How to Make Yourself a Body without Organs," an entire chapter written in the second person – literally an instruction manual for exploring "continuums of intensities segment by segment" (Deleuze & Guattari 1987, 161).

The exhortatory mood continues in the famous chapter on "Becoming-Intense, Becoming-Animal, Becoming-Imperceptible ... " Becoming-animal, however, is removed from the ethological picture of animality Deleuze sketched out in his work on Spinoza a decade earlier. Instead, the animal is subsumed under a Bergsonian emphasis on the *different-in-kind* locus of *becoming* as such. Spinoza appears, but is primarily invoked as a theorist of the plane of immanence on which all formations of substance play out: "A fixed plan of life upon which everything stirs, slows down or accelerates. A single abstract Animal for all the assemblages that effectuate it" (Deleuze & Guattari 1987, 255). The shift from ethology – an attention to concrete animals in their specificity – to a "single abstract Animal" underlines how far the conceptual center of gravity of Deleuze's work has shifted away from a sensitivity to how biology and philosophy might constructively interact.

The chapter is set up as a polemic against structuralism, and in particular structuralist models of doing history, which effectively inoculates the world against what Deleuze and Guattari identify as *becomings*, or the emergence of radical novelty, new lines of flight away from existing series. In a section entitled "Memories of a Bergsonian," Deleuze and Guattari write "[w]e believe in the existence of very special becomings-animal traversing human beings and sweeping them away, affecting the animal no less than the human" (Deleuze & Guattari 1987, 237). For Deleuze and Guattari, a becoming is not simply a transformation or imitation. In a transformation, one could say, the emphasis is on the finished product. Instead, for Deleuze and Guattari, "[b]ecoming produces nothing other than itself" (Deleuze & Guattari 1987, 238). The focal point of becoming is the modality of change as such, rather than what one changes into. This is phrased in Bergsonian terms as a *difference in kind*: there is "a reality specific to becoming (the Bergsonian idea of a coexistence of very different 'durations,' superior or inferior to 'ours,' all of them in communication)" (Deleuze & Guattari 1987, 238). Whereas the "Memories of a Spinozist" emphasize the continuous plane of immanence, the "Memories of a Bergsonian" point to a qualitative difference in kind in which becoming lands orthogonally to the plane of immanence.

Deleuze and Guattari aren't trying to introduce actual animals here. They assert that animals undergo becomings just like humans, but their real interest is in animals on the mythic register. The emphasis is on the passage from a molar subject to a molecular subject – the decompositions of an organized system of elements into something that is displaced, dissociated, and undone. The same applies to the chain of equivalencies Deleuze and Guattari draw between becoming-animal and all other forms of becoming – becoming-woman, becoming-child (Deleuze & Guattari 1987, 248). *Woman* and *child* are just as abstract as *animal*.[3] Deleuze and Guattari seem to recognize that they have left a theory of power behind them. "It is of course," they write, "indispensable for women to conduct a molar politics, with a view to winning back their own organism, their own history, their own subjectivity" (Deleuze & Guattari 1987, 276). Rhapsodizing of the displaced and marginalized aside, becoming-majoritarian is indispensable for guaranteeing rights, safety, and security.

Crucially, however, the molar-molecular divide manifests two neat philosophical effects that profoundly shape the interpretation of Deleuze. On the one hand, it finalizes a merger between Bergson and Deleuze. Bergson's conceptual structure (creative emotion) leading to a spectral dualism is clear, but it is now fully cloaked in Deleuze's vocabulary (affects). On the other, it fully erases the emphasis in Spinoza on *affects*, as distinguished from *affections* (though Deleuze and Guattari have swapped their meanings). The hymn to minoritarianism insists that the anomalous individual who represents the fullest flowering of becoming "has only affects, it has neither familiar or subjectified feelings, nor specific or significant characteristics" (Deleuze & Guattari 1987, 244). Spinoza's affect/emotions such as compassion, shame, and thankfulness – things we can feel, above the bounding line of "consciousness" – have been banished. The structure of *creative emotion* as the manifestation of becoming, that which is different in kind from the sequence of perception-object-matter, is clearly visible, though its name has been changed. The implications of this surgical extrication of emotion for thinking politics will be explored further below.

In sum, within Deleuze's philosophy we can see a tension between a relentless monism in Spinoza's work – one that posits continuity between matter and mind, the micro and the macro – and a sophisticated spectral dualism that locates affectivity in a dimension apart from the material. I think, on some

---

[3] See Haraway 2008, 27 for a development of this line of criticism.

level, Deleuze and Guattari know that "Memoirs of a Bergsonian" and "Memoirs of a Spinozist" don't quite mesh. But they insist on a sort of mystical genre in which all contradictions are reconciled, rather than signaling that they're creating a new piece of philosophical armature designed to connect disparate thinkers. There are, no doubt, artful maneuvers available to try to perfectly reconcile these divergent tonalities in Deleuze's thought. (As we will see below, Brian Massumi sees this as one of his tasks.) I suggest that it is equally plausible that Deleuze, like all expansive, groundbreaking thinkers, contained multitudes, and that a harmonic reconciliation would artificially laminate his fundamentally shardlike body of thought.

Deleuze in Affect Theory

Deleuze's main advocate in the development of a theory of affect has been Brian Massumi. Massumi's resumé includes not only one of the first handbooks of Deleuze and Guattari's work, but the standard English translation of *A Thousand Plateaus*. In Massumi's 1995 essay "The Autonomy of Affect" (republished in his 2002 volume *Parables for the Virtual*) he develops a set of Deleuzian motifs into a programmatic vocabulary of affect. In particular, Massumi expands the Bergsonian line of Deleuze's thought (and Guattari's, though I'll just refer to the former from here on out), arguing for a distinction between *affect* as a register of intensity and *emotions* as structured, static forms available to consciousness.

Massumi builds this argument, in part, with reference to scientific studies. He cites a pair of famous experiment by the researcher Benjamin Libet. In the first, subjects were administered an electrical pulse, either to a brain-implanted electrode or to the skin. The subjects could only feel the pulse, it was determined, if the pulse lasted at least half a second. In the second experiment, subjects were wired to an electroencephalograph (EEG), a neurometric machine that translates brain activity into signals recorded by an inked needle that leaves marks on a scrolling sheet of paper. The subjects were placed in front of a clocklike device mounted on the wall showing a quickly rotating dot, then asked to flex a finger, while also noting the position of the dot. Comparing the EEG output with their report of *when they announced their decision*, it was discovered that brain activity spiked 0.3 seconds before the decision, and the action took place 0.2 seconds after they clocked their decision. In other words, there seemed to be activity upstream of conscious decision-making.

Massumi quotes Libet as concluding from this experiment that "we may exert free will not by initiating intentions but by vetoing, acceding, or otherwise responding to them after they arise" (in Massumi 2002, 29). Massumi rephrases this in Bergsonian terms: "the half second is missed not because it is empty, but because it is overfull, in excess of the actually-performed action and of its ascribed meaning. Will and consciousness are *subtractive*. They are *limitative, derived functions* that reduce a complexity too rich to be functionally expressed" (Massumi 2002, 29). For Massumi, this provides compelling evidence for the Bergsonian picture of affect as a radically open field that is reduced by consciousness into a finite stream of awareness.

Another scientific witness brought by Massumi: an experiment in which the Austrian researcher Hertha Sturm and her team showed children a series of short films about a melting snowman. The films had been overlaid with different voice tracks: the first was wordless, the second offered a matter-of-fact running commentary, like a news report, and the third offered a commentary on the emotional tenor of the scenes. The children were asked to rate the films according to their "pleasantness." They found the matter-of-fact voiceover least pleasant, and the original, wordless version most pleasant. They were then asked to rate the individual scenes on the scales of "happy-sad" and "pleasant-unpleasant." This is where the signal finding for Massumi came out: it turned out that the children rated the *saddest scenes* the *most pleasant*: "the sadder the better" (Massumi 2002, 23, emphasis original).

Massumi's conclusion is that although the emotion "sadness" is bad, the affective preconditions of the emotion are what actually motivate bodies to want to watch the film. Massumi sees this finding as evidence of the perpendicularly interlocked planes of "signifying order and intensity" (Massumi 2002, 24). "Intensity is qualifiable as an emotional state," he suggests,

> and that state is static – temporal and narrative noise. It is a state of suspense, potentially of disruption. It is like a temporal sink, a hole in time, as we conceive of it and narrativize it. It is not exactly passivity, because it is filled with motion, vibratory motion, resonation. And it is not yet activity, because the motion is not of the kind that can be directed (if only symbolically) toward practical ends in a world of constituted objects and aims (if only on screen). (Massumi 2002, 26)

It is this register of intensity that Massumi correlates with affect, the pure zone of possibility that forms the background coordinates of experience, but that is in principle undetectable on the register of experience. Intensities – affects – leave traces as emotions as they *escape* bodies, but they can never be known or experienced in and of themselves.

This is because affects are, Massumi argues, the fully *autonomous* register of becoming: affect does not exist except inasmuch as it chases the horizon line of the virtual becoming actual. "The autonomy of affect," Massumi writes, "is its participation in the virtual. *Its autonomy is its openness*. Affect is autonomous to the degree to which it escapes confinement in the particular body whose vitality, or potential for interaction, it is" (Massumi 2002, 35). As Ann Pellegrini and Jasbir Puar put it, "[t]his conception of affect poses a distinction between sensation and the perception of the sensation. Affect, from this perspective, is precisely what allows the body to be an open system, always in concert with its virtuality, the potential of becoming" (Pellegrini & Puar 2009, 37).

Whereas Spinoza emphasized a continuum of substance from the micro register to the macro, from *affections* (the play of substance) to *affects* (named emotions) – a theme developed in at least some of Deleuze's work – the dominant tone of Massumi's interpretation is the Bergsonian motif. Massumi identifies his task as finishing and formalizing Deleuze's synchronization of Spinoza and Bergson (Massumi 2002, 32). He makes the claim that Spinoza is interested in a recursive "excluded middle" as the moment of "emergence" of mind from body. "Spinoza's ethics," he proposes, "is the philosophy of the becoming-active, in parallel, of mind and body, from an origin in passion, in impingement, in so pure and productive a receptivity that it can only be conceived as a third state, an excluded middle, prior to the distinction between activity and passivity: affect" (Massumi 2002, 32). It's beyond the scope of this work to delve into what Spinoza really means and the extent to which he can be harmonized with Bergson. It's enough for my purposes to show that this move of linking the Bergsonian and Spinozist lines is speculative in Deleuze, and highly contestable in Massumi.[4] But it explains the emphasis, in Massumi's work, on an orthogonal relationship between intersecting planes representing difference in kind, rather than continuity. True affect is always only obliquely related to experience, but experience is itself directed by this turbulent welter of becomings.

This model necessitated, for Massumi, the abandonment of earlier phenomenological research into sensing bodies: "they were difficult to reconcile with the new understandings of the structuring capacities of culture and their inseparability both from the exercise of power and the glimmers of counterpower incumbent in mediate living. [Phenomenology] was all about a subject without subjectivism: a subject 'constructed' by external mechanisms. 'The Subject'" (Massumi 2002, 2). The subject of phenomenology – what Massumi sees as a rigid, static ontology, the congealed residue of becomings – dissolves and is

---

[4] Other readers of Deleuze, such as Michael Hardt (1993) stress a different set of features within Spinoza's thought in order to reconcile him with Bergson and justify Deleuze's interpretation. This move tends to correlate with an increased emphasis on Spinoza as a resource for thinking about the play of being and becoming as such, which, I would argue, still fails to connect to a meaningful theory of power.

replaced by an analytics of anti-structure, a chain of terms that are all predicates of the phenomenological subject but are ultimately unavailable to it: "Affect, sensation, perception, movement, intensity, tendency, habit, law, chaos, recursion, relation, immanence, the 'feedback of higher forms.' Emergence, becoming, history, space, time, space-time, space and time as emergences" (Massumi 2002, 16).

The Deleuzian Dialect on Power

This chain of concepts becomes the foundation for Massumi's version of the analytics of power. In this version of affect theory, the scintillation of the stream of becoming functions as the currency of power. Affect, Massumi writes, "holds a key to rethinking postmodern power after ideology. For although ideology is still very much with us, often in the most virulent of forms, it is no longer encompassing" (Massumi 2002, 42). In other words, the operation of an ideology – a field of interlocking discourses designed to mask present material circumstances as unbending truth – is no longer sufficient for understanding power. This passage seems to be worded to suggest that the nature of power itself has changed in the "postmodern" condition, an interpretation corroborated by Massumi's later comment on the defeat of President Bill Clinton's health care plan in the 1990s, as evidence of the idea that "affect is a real condition, an intrinsic variable of the late capitalist system, as infrastructural as a factory" (Massumi 2002, 45). Affect, then, as a feature of power, is something that is uniquely correlated to the contemporary cultural condition. This has everything to do with affect's distinct property of transmissibility through media networks: affective "atoms," Massumi writes, "are autonomous not through closure but through a singular openness" (Massumi 2002, 43). As affects track the force of becoming, they translate into streams of power. Politics can be affective, or not-affective, depending on your tactical preference.

This is the tool used by Massumi in his famous analysis of Ronald Reagan's political effectiveness. For Massumi, the politician's face is a node of power. In a third scientific specimen case, Massumi draws on the research of the neuroscientist Oliver Sacks. Sacks describes being in a hospital ward with a group of patients, some suffering from aphasia (an impairment in grasping the meaning of words, compensated for by acute development of the ability to read facial expressions and gestures), others from tonal agnosia (difficulty registering tones of voice, leading to hyper-attention to linguistic and grammatical form of sentences). The TV set on the ward was tuned to Reagan, then president, giving a speech. The speech had an unexpected effect: it provoked howls of laughter from both groups. Sacks' conclusion was that Reagan was not using a coherent mesh of words and facial expressions: his facial expressions were exaggerated and bizarre, while his speech was fragmentary and nonsensical.

Massumi argues that Reagan's ability to marshal a national political network emerged from exactly this arrangement of his bodily gestures and expressions in an *oblique* relationship to the propositional content of his policy positions. "Reagan politicized the power of mime," he writes. "A mime decomposes movement, cuts its continuity into a potentially infinite series of submovements punctuated by jerks. At each jerk, at each cut into the movement, the *potential* is there for the movement to veer off in another direction, to *become* a different movement" (Massumi 2002, 40, my emphasis). Reagan tuned his body and speech to the frequency of pure becoming. His "gestural idiocy had a mime effect. As did his verbal incoherence in the register of meaning" (Massumi 2002, 41). It was by commandeering the stream of becoming – not by mastering cogent arguments – that Reagan was able to rise. This is the theory of power offered by affect theory in the dialect of Deleuze: it locates the ability to make bodies move in the register of becoming.

We can find no shortage of examples of this correlation of affect (qua becoming) to power in the Deleuzian affect theory literature. Erin Manning uses it to theorize biopolitics in her book *Relationscapes*. Manning makes explicit that her work follows the cues of Bergson in stressing "the virtual force of movement's taking form" (Manning 2009, 6). A body, she contends, operates as a node of affect because it is a "pure plastic rhythm" (Manning 2009, 6). This makes the body an open thing, a horizon for transformation "that resists predefinition in terms of subjectivity or identity, a body that is involved in a reciprocal reaching-toward that in-gathers the world even as it worlds" (Manning 2009, 6). Affect is that which "moves, constituting the event that, in many cases, becomes-body" (Manning 2013, 5). The body susceptible to radical becoming – a node of weather patterns – is the operative term.

This leads to Manning's template for thinking about Foucault's concept of biopolitics. She proposes that biopolitics can be understood as "a series that works conjunctively with the notion of the disciplined individual while it moves beyond it toward a body-becoming" (Manning 2009, 138).[5] In her analysis of the Nazi filmmaker Leni Riefenstahl she develops a new concept, the *biogram*: an image of a body in a state of becoming. This image, she proposes, has the capacity to open a new channel of biopolitical force. Riefenstahl's images of dynamic bodies create "not a body as such but an affective tone of a becoming-body, a plastic rhythm, a transcendent materiality, a topological surface,

---

[5] Manning suggests that this is Foucault's definition, but without citation. To the best of my knowledge *becoming* in the Deleuzian sense does not appear in Foucault's late works.

a physically transcendent asignifying materiality" (Manning 2009, 141). The rhythmic sequencing of these images of bodies in a state of becoming is the liquid form of power; it makes "politics begin to move" (Manning 2009, 141).

Zizi Papacharissi also takes cues from the Deleuzian dialect in her work, such as *Affective Publics*. Although she is less committed to a crystalline break between affect and emotion, at least at the level of vocabulary, she shares a sense that

> [d]isorder, marginality, and anarchy present the habitat for affect, mainly because order, mainstreaming, and hierarchy afford form that compromises the futurity of affect. Because marginal spaces support the emergence of change, affect is inherently political, although it does not conform to the structures we symbolically internalize as political. Thus, per affect theory, empowerment lies in liminality, in pre-emergence and emergence, or at the point at which new formations of the political are in the process of being imagined but not yet articulated. The form of affective power is *pre-actualized, networked*, and of a *liquid nature*. (Papacharissi 2015, 19, emphasis added)

As with Massumi, as with Bergson, Papacharissi locates affect in a realm outside of structure. Power is channeled by resonating with this "liquid" affect.

By unravelling order and hierarchy, affect transforms political contexts. This leads into Papacharissi's sustained case study in this book: "networked digital structures of expression and connection," which she argues "are overwhelmingly characterized by affect" (Papacharissi 2015, 8). As with Massumi's analysis of Reaganism, affect is a property that a political strategy either *has or does not have*. Media forms "democratize by inviting a turn to the affective" (Papacharissi 2015, 25). Papacharissi is more sunny than Massumi about affect, seeming to gravitate toward examples where media technology – a student-built radio station during the uprising against the military junta in Greece in 1973, Twitter and Facebook during the Arab Spring – effectively focused pressure on oppressive regimes, but her framing of affect remains on the register of becoming.

Massumi recapitulates this model of power when he turns his attention to animality in his 2014 book *What Animals Teach Us about Politics*. Massumi interprets animality through the prism of Gregory Bateson's notion of *play*, which he sees as an outgrowth of instinct. But where the conventional sense of instinct is as something fixed, Massumi insists that it is better understood as *variable*. Instinct, he suggests, is a path of improvisation. It "always has a first degree of appetitive mentality, a hunger for the supernormal, however weighed down and laid low it may be with inherited corporeality and its penchant for sameness" (Massumi 2014, 32). This quality of becoming amplifies the survival

profile of an animal organism, which through improvisation manages to out-
maneuver predators or better exploit resources in its environment (Massumi
2014, 13). Play is the field within which actions are shaped by excess intensity –
the vitality affect of becoming (Massumi 2014, 28).

Massumi takes this notion of play as a zone of becoming and transposes it
into the analytics of power. What he calls *animal politics* he characterizes as "a
politics of becoming, even – especially – of the human" (Massumi 2014, 50).
Concluding in a normative key, Massumi writes that a properly animal politics
"does not recognize the wisdom of utility as the criterion of good conduct.
Rather, it affirms ludic excess. It does not cleave to the golden mean. It
excessively lives out the in-between" (Massumi 2014, 39). Animal politics
is the politics of Reagan and beyond: it's the ensemble of mechanisms
circulating power by jump-cutting, distributing becomings, and pulling bodies
along in their wake. In Massumi's terms, it is "a politics of the performative
gesture, alloying itself with practices of improvisational and participative art
in the wild" (Massumi 2014, 40). Politics works, Massumi writes, to "the
degree to which the political gesture carries forward enthusiasm of the body"
(Massumi 2014, 41). Power is liquidated into a pure stream of affective
becoming.

The Deleuzian dialect of affect theory, then, offers a way of studying not just
thought and experience, but the operation of power itself. Massumi's framing is
particularly useful for identifying the thick channels of power running outside
of language. Why *was* Reagan so effective as a politician given the incoherence
of so much of his speech – a condition even more astonishing with a figure like
Donald Trump? How do images – like a politician's face – emerge as nodes that
come to conduct bodies in conjunction with systems of power? How do media
platforms – without saying a word – spark abrupt political transformations?
Why *do* we love music without words? Massumi offers a vision of affect theory
as a theory of the ways we are moved without words – even without concepts –
a theory of *where bodies go*, and so a theory of power. As I have argued
elsewhere, the model of power that focuses exclusively on discourse as the
medium for the transmission of power succumbs to the *linguistic fallacy*: the
fiction advanced by some critical strands in the humanities that humans are
fundamentally linguistic-cognitive beings and that the things that move us must
also be fundamentally linguistic-cognitive (Schaefer 2015). Massumi's contribution is to show that power "feels" before it thinks.

At the same time, the version of affect theory that enshrines Bergsonian
spectral dualism, with its attendant understanding of affect as *different in kind*
from bodies, brings with it a number of liabilities. These are visible in the
engagement between the Deleuzian dialect and science, but also play out as

a pressing set of problems with the Deleuzian model of power. As Sara Ahmed has written, in presupposing a bright line between the "personal" and the "pre-personal," the "analytic distinction between affect and emotion risks cutting emotions off from the lived experiences of being and having a body" (Ahmed 2004b, 39, en. 4). The next section considers these criticisms in greater detail, en route to developing an account of affect more attentive to the nexus between formations of power and embodied life.

2 Unbecoming: Criticisms of the Deleuzian Dialect of Affect Theory

Brian Massumi's work has been subject to a number of criticisms, many of them converging on his evocation of a set of scientific data points. In this section, I want to explore the range of these criticisms, beginning with the work of Ruth Leys, who has written extensively on what she sees as the weaknesses of affect theory. Building on a line of criticism developed by Constantina Papoulias and Felicity Callard, I will explore the liabilities of conceptualizing affect as becoming by introducing perspectives in the life sciences, particularly with reference to the contemporary Extended Evolutionary Synthesis. I will conclude with criticisms of affect as becoming offered by other affect theorists, such as Eve Kosofsky Sedgwick. This will set the stage for a deeper consideration of Sedgwick's work – and in particular Sedgwick's interest in the work of Silvan Tomkins – in the next section. Rather than starting with the autonomy of affect, this will lead us to a sense of affect theory that begins with its animality.

The Critique of Anti-intentionalism

The most determined critic of affect theory to date is the historian and trauma theorist Ruth Leys. Leys' essay "The Turn to Affect: A Critique" and the book it generated, *The Ascent of Affect: Genealogy and Critique,* are widely cited by critics dissatisfied with certain aspects of affect theory. Taking on a decades-long debate within the psychology of emotions, Leys' primary argument is against a certain *anti-intentionalist* strand of the conversation that suggests felt states can be objectless. But she is upfront that the genesis of this concern lay in her frustration with cultural critics such as Massumi and Sedgwick (Leys 2017, 24). I want to engage with Leys' criticisms in detail to clarify where my own line of analysis converges with and diverges from hers. Moreover, highlighting some of the shortcomings of Leys' account will clarify what's at stake in conceptualizing affect theory, animality, and power as intimately associated.

Leys has a number of criticisms of affect theory as a field, some of which I will cover here, some in the section "The Animality of Affect". She spends a significant amount of time responding to Massumi's work, and in particular, his use of the Libet and Sturm experiments. A trained historian of science, she provides an impressive range of scientific and philosophical pushback on Libet's experimental setup and his conclusions. For instance, scientists commenting on Libet's initial 1985 publication noted that Libet had designed his experiment in such a way as to compel participants to do something that fell outside the pattern of ordinary action – namely, to pay *conscious* attention to their actions. Citing the philosopher Shaun Gallagher, she points out that Libet's experiment therefore puts subjects in the position of patients who have suffered damage to their nervous system and must chain together a conscious intent with a physical action, rather than simulating a neurotypical experience of one's own actions (Leys 2017, 327).

Leys' objective is to show that Massumi's inference from these results – that the genesis of action is located upstream of conscious awareness – is flawed. She's especially concerned about one of the philosophical ramifications of taking this position: "a classical dualism of mind and body informs both Libet's and Massumi's shared interpretation of Libet's experimental findings," she points out, before continuing, "it is only by adopting a highly idealized or metaphysical picture of the mind as completely separate from the body and brain to which it freely directs its intentions and decisions that they can reach the skeptical conclusions they do" (Leys 2017, 326). This may or may not be a spectral dualism. One could imagine an argument that, like Deleuze in his interpretation of Bergson, this dualism eventually reconciles itself into a deeper monism. But nonetheless, it is a device that insists on imposing *difference in kind* on a complex relationship. Rather than seeing the body and consciousness as existing in a state of radical continuity, as Spinoza did, Leys has detected a fissure that has been opened between them. In other words, Leys has, in essence, retraced the Bergsonian schism in Deleuze's thought as it has been passed down through Massumi.

In her critique of Massumi's use of Sturm's experiments showing films of melting snowmen to children, Leys develops a similar theme, though in this case she absolves the experimenter of responsibility (this experiment having received significantly less commentary than Libet's) and primarily attacks Massumi's interpretation:

> It is important to notice that Massumi imposes on Sturm's experimental findings an interpretation motivated by a set of assumptions about the asignifying nature of affect. These assumptions drive his analysis of Sturm's data in order to produce a distinction between, on the one hand, the conscious, signifying ('emotional' and intellectual) processes held to be captive to the fixity of received meanings and categories, and on the other hand, the nonconscious affective processes of intensity held to be autonomous from signification. (Leys 2017, 322)

It's the Bergson trap again, the observation that Massumi consistently invokes a spectral dualism that separates conscious and preconscious domains. At the same time, Leys' criticisms here are less compelling than her case file against the Libet experiment. Massumi may well find material for thinking through his own particular conceptual vocabulary in this case study. But that is not an argument against him. Theories always emerge in a dynamic dance with data and the Sturm experiment seems to serve as an effective illustration of at least one facet of Massumi's argument.

More importantly, Leys overplays her hand when she argues that Massumi is too invested in the idea that feeling and intensity could be located on orthogonal axes: "are not sad films sometimes also pleasurable or enjoyable?" she asks, dismissing Massumi's analysis as trivial (Leys 2017, 319). But Leys's appeal here misses the forest for the trees. The fact that sad films are experienced as pleasant is exactly the philosophical puzzle that Massumi is trying to explain. Leys overlooks what makes Massumi's analysis so interesting: the puzzle of how we are pulled – in unexpected and unanticipated ways – into decisions, situations, and formations of power.

Leys' valid point that Massumi lapses into spectral dualism could, then, be applied to her own framework. "The whole point of the turn to affect by Massumi," she contends, "is to shift attention away from considerations of meaning or 'ideology' or indeed representation to the subject's subpersonal material-affective responses, where, it is claimed, political and other influences do their real work" (Leys 2017, 322). This leads to her assertion that for Massumi and other affect theorists, "what is crucial is not your beliefs and intentions but the affective processes that are said to produce them, with the result that political change becomes a matter not of persuading others of the truth of your ideas but of producing new ontologies or 'becomings,' new bodies, and new lives" (Leys 2017, 343). She insists that the fact that we are "embodied, affective creatures" has no "implications whatsoever for determining whether or not particular beliefs or opinions are true, or even worth taking seriously" (Leys 2017, 348).

Leys's affirmation of intentionalism is, at its heart, a way of rehearsing a political ontology that insists that the only correct way to understand power and to participate in political action is in a public sphere of properly vetted reasons. For Leys, as for Massumi, *the issue is consciousness*. Where Massumi wants to locate the substance of subjectivity upstream of consciousness, Leys insists on finding it in a fully conscious, reasoning subject adjudicating true and false. Her concern seems to be with the way the affect theory approach "marginalizes the intact person with his or her intentions and meanings" (Leys 2017, 16). For Leys as well, then, there is a necessity of dualism. Both she and

Massumi assume a thing called consciousness; they only differ in whether what matters for subjectivity lies above or below the water-line. (I will consider below the possibility that pinning so much of their analysis to a nebulous, poorly defined metaphysical category like consciousness is exactly what sets up the unending and unproductive battle tableau between them.)

This leads into a startling bait and switch, in which Leys abruptly drops all reference to Massumi in the final pages of *Ascent of Affect* and instead offers Jane Bennett's 2010 book *Vibrant Matter* as an illustration of the failures of affect theory to diagnose political situations. Bennett's claim in this book is that macro-level events need to be considered in part as effects of material forces that are themselves best understood as agents. Leys is swift to mock this claim: "Her fantasy is rather of a language of nature that isn't itself a representation because it consists of material vibrations or neural currents by which the affects are inevitably passed on, though not exactly understood" (Leys 2017, 349).

The rapid rail-jumping of Leys' line of thought masks a significant gap in her argument. On the one hand, she has slammed together two thinkers who, while sharing a commitment to working out different aspects of Deleuze's thought, are very different. Massumi writes little about matter, being far more interested in the register of the virtual. Bennett, for her part, writes little about affects in their felt sense, and not at all about becoming.[6] They are, in other words, writing about power in very different registers. More to the point, Leys cherry-picks one of Bennett's examples (the active role of the power grid in a blackout), while ignoring Massumi's case studies of affect in politics entirely. She doesn't mention Massumi's problematic but thought-provoking account of how political power is conducted affectively – the question of how a political movement can come to be organized around a politician's face rather than a set of reasoned political positions, for instance. We may well wish for a political sphere ruled by reason. But we need tools to explain why we don't have it yet. And if we conclude that the absence of a radically reasonable public sphere is a permanent feature of our social existence, we need even more tools to learn how to navigate the world we're left with.

Leys is correct to put pressure on certain features of Massumi's thought – the logic of spectral dualism that locates affect in a register of becoming, fundamentally distinct from bodies – a line of criticism I will develop further in the next section. But she misses the significance of his thought as a resource for thinking about power, for thinking about the way bodies are reticulated into

---

[6] Bennett doesn't cite Massumi or any of Leys' other *bêtes noires* – Sedgwick, Tomkins, or Ekman – in this book, with the notable exception of William Connolly. Bennett explicitly identifies her understanding of affect as "Spinozist," suggesting that she has not made the Bergsonian turn which is so central to Massumi's thought (Bennett 2010, xii).

political formations on the multiplicity of registers that exceed rational debate. Ultimately, her argument is no different from the accusation levied against "postmodernism" for generations: a characterization of its account of *how meaning is made within contingent histories* as an act of sinister sabotage against Truth. As Carolyn Pedwell writes, her "sweeping claims seem more indicative of anxieties within philosophical and political thought concerning a possible loss of the authority traditionally attached to 'reasoned argument', than they do of the state of the art within interdisciplinary affect and emotion studies" (Pedwell forthcoming, n.p.). And it misses the way that affect theory seeks to move beyond the postmodern fixation on the polysemy of representation – the endless play of signification and spirals of meaning – to a more textured account of how bodies work.

Criticisms of the Deleuzian Dialect from the Life Sciences

A more promising line of criticism of the Deleuzian dialect is offered by Constantina Papoulias and Felicity Callard. Papoulias and Callard take a narrower focus on the use of *specific* neuroscientists in affect theory, rather than trying to derive a line of attack from the vast, deeply complex half-century debate about intentionality in psychology. They link Massumi's "Autonomy of Affect" essay to culture critic Mark Hansen, finding in both a commitment to an "afoundational biologism," a selective reading that frames the insights of the life sciences – including neuroscience – exclusively in terms of fluidity and openness. Affect, in this sense, reflects the capacity for radical transformation, "the body's foundational dimension of creativity . . . a conduit for the transformative potentiality of lived experience" (Papoulias & Callard 2010, 35). Habit, ideology, and oppressive political machines can all be overwhelmed by the electrifying force of affect.

What Papoulias and Callard show, however, is that far from stressing plasticity, the neurosciences thematize a more complex interaction between plastic and stereotyped behaviors resulting from brain architecture. The neuroscientist Antonio Damasio, for instance, is often invoked as a figure pointing to the precognitive foundations of subjectivity. Without disputing Damasio's model, Papoulias and Callard argue that this tips in the direction of *behavioral and affective rigidity* rather than becoming. Whereas Deleuze sees in affect an open system susceptible to radical transformation, neuroscientists emphasize that "the body's non-cognitive dimension is at least in part pre-adapted to initiate very precise, *constrained* courses of action (such as running away from certain types of stimulus)," which is actually illustrative of "the *intransigence* of emotional conditioning" (Papoulias & Callard 2010, 41, my emphasis).

Damasio's research, for instance, demonstrates not the radical potentialization of the brain, but the brain as a material structure that configures consciousness in relatively inflexible ways depending on its attributes (Damasio 1994; 1999).

There is, then, a disconnect between affect understood, on the one hand, as Spinoza's *affections* – a set of properties of substance that interlink all things, including mind and matter (and eventually scale up into emotion-like *affects*) – and, on the other hand, as Bergson's *virtual* as a register of becoming that is in principle immune to capture. Papoulias and Callard propose that in the neuroscience picture, *becoming* is unworkable as a model of embodied affect. This is why the correlation of affect to an "emancipatory script" in some versions of affect theory stressing a convergence between affect and liberation – an interpretation carrying forward Deleuze's own romantic tendencies – falls apart (Papoulias & Callard 2010, 47).

One way of spotlighting this mistake is to look at the way Massumi understands the category of instinct. For Massumi, "instinctual movements are animated by a tendency to surpass given forms . . . they are moved by an impetus toward creativity" (Massumi 2014, 17). From a biological perspective, this is a difficult claim to make sense of. It's not wrong that instinct is more than just stereotyped movement. Many zoologists have seen fit to abandon the notion of instinct altogether as too much in hock to a notion of animal minds as mechanical – the nonintellectual other to glorious human reason (de Waal 2005, 147). But the most interesting part of whatever-instinct-is isn't that it sometimes varies. It's that it so often remains the same. Instincts – probably better understood as durable learning rules that are embedded in the phenotypes of animal minds – are semi-stable bodily processes that recur with remarkable consistency across populations and generations of a single species. Their locus can't really be explained by an ontology of becoming.

Instead, they diagram a subtle but intransigent tissue of mental protocols that shape subjectivity. Massumi proposes that the tendency of instincts to exceed themselves is "an evolutionary advantage" (Massumi 2014, 18). Not every evolved feature is adaptive (see Gould 2002), but if we're going to speculate on fitness benefits, the *fixity* of certain instincts – stereotyped motions, desires, and forms – needs to be seen as having adaptive benefits. It is precisely because intricate macro-organisms like us must interact with the world in sophisticated ways that we have intransigent learning biases in the first place. All animals have predispositions to interact with the world in particular ways, from locomotion to feeding to reproduction. Humans are different from other mammals in the *degree* to which our behaviors tend to be learned rather than prefixed – the difference between a highly altricial (requiring sustained nourishment) and a highly precocial (maturing rapidly) organism. This is both the source of human success and a potential vulnerability. A 3-month-old doe is far better equipped to navigate the world on her own than a 3-year-old human (3-year-old humans being notoriously unhelpful when it comes to the business of getting by in the world). Rigid "instinct," in this sense, is advantageous not because it can modulate itself, but because it implements a beneficial *repetitive* relationship between the organism and its environment.

Although cognitive flexibility among some large-brained macro-organisms adds a new dimension to fitness, semi-stable biological and psychological features embedded in organisms at birth or early in development – like knowing the smells of certain predators or to root for a nipple – are the core survival strategy at the level of every animal organism with a brain (Panksepp 1998, 55; see also Breland & Breland 1961). Without these mental forms, animals would have no way of differentiating the collection of things in their environment – *food, threats, mates* – leaving us in a position comparable to microorganisms, bouncing off everything in the world and hoping for the best (Margulis 1998, 111). This same stability of learning rules is equally necessary at the level of physiology. From a biological perspective, becoming will kill you. The best prescription for general health is for our intricately structured organs, cells, and tissues to keep *becoming* to an absolute minimum, by and large being exactly the same boring old *beings* day after day.

The same could be said of our brain chemistry. Although neuroscientists differ in their assessment of the extent to which the brain is specialized according to particular locations and circuits as opposed to the extent to which it is generalized, or *equipotent*, there is broad agreement that certain parts of the brain do different things.[7] At the level of the chemical relay system used to transmit information between neurons, neurotransmitters are molecules with a distinct structure that function because they bond to a finely tuned receptor structure in the receiving neuron. This system is so effective that it is almost entirely intact across the mammalian world (Panksepp 1998, 100). Some basic neurotransmitters are even shared with invertebrates: "Even the endorphins that made my labor pains tolerable," Sarah Blaffer Hrdy writes, "came from molecules that humans still share with earthworms" (Hrdy 1999, xv).

This is why an opioid epidemic is so catastrophic: opioids mimic the structure of endorphins, bonding to their receptors and sharply distorting the way the body experiences pleasure and pain. Because morphine was discovered long before endorphins were identified in the 1970s, *endorphin* is itself a contraction of *endogenous morphine*, that is to say, the morphine-like substance in the brain. For the same reason, Darwin was able to make the argument in *The Descent of*

---

[7] See Barrett (2017), chapter 1.

Man that humans and other animals must be on a single continuum of development because "[m]edicines [produce] the same effect on them as on us. Many kinds of monkeys have a strong taste for tea, coffee, and spirituous liquors: they will also, as I have myself seen, smoke tobacco with pleasure" (Darwin 1882, 7). *Becoming* is not an operative mechanism here: it is the *fixity* of neurotransmitters that makes them work. Should they start changing their molecular structure into forms unrecognizable to receiving neurons, it will be the functional equivalent of a kill-switch in our brains.

A similar kind of error is made in the way that Massumi conceptualizes evolution itself. For Massumi, evolution, too, is an ecstatic moment that can be understood in Bergsonian terms. The improvisational "power of expressive mentality" is, for Bergson, "the very engine of evolution, responsible for inventing the forms that come to be selected as adaptive" (Massumi 2014, 14). Evolution itself is best understood, in this view, as "a continual variation across recurrent iterations, repeating the splay always with a difference" (Massumi 2014, 14). Our link with animality is bonded by a chain of becomings – zaps of improvisation injecting novelty in the structure of organic life.

This is not wrong, in a sense, but it is trivial, in the same way that one could say that the *you* of now and the *you* of 20 minutes ago are linked by a series of accidental becomings that make you the slightly different *you* that you are now. Becoming adds nothing to our basic sense of micrological change over time. The problem is that the emphasis on becoming washes out what is most interesting about evolution, namely, the *dynamic between change and continuity* – the way that certain fixed elements are picked up, replaced, relocated, and remixed with other fixed elements. There is novelty within the system, but a total constitution by novelty would not produce evolution: it would produce noise. In order for something as sophisticated as an organism to emerge, there needs to be a robust conservation of form, in dynamic relation with transformation.

This is well illustrated in the emerging conversations about the proposed Extended Evolutionary Synthesis (EES), led by philosophers of biology such as Massimo Pigliucci. Proponents of the EES see it as a way to take the Modern Evolutionary Synthesis (devised in the first half of the twentieth century when Mendelian genetics were applied to solve problems within Darwin's framework of evolution by natural selection), and expand it to include new problems and concerns that have emerged in subsequent research, such as epigenetics and niche construction. As Pigliucci and Gerd B. Muller argue, the EES can be understood as a new emphasis on a "causal-mechanistic approach in evolutionary theory," the underpinning of which is "a hugely expanded knowledge base consisting of large data sets in genetics, development, plasticity, inheritance, and other empirical domains" (Pigliucci & Müller 2010, 12). Genes as molecules are not just nodes of information. They have a distinct micro-physical structure. This structure dictates how, for instance, proteins affected by these genes are developed and organized. Mutation of genes, transposition of chromosomes, and epigenetic factors that reshape the expression of genes are all *mechanical* processes interfacing with these molecules in specific ways.

The foundation of this problem was already present in Darwin's theory. One of the most astute criticisms of evolution by natural selection in the nineteenth century came from a Scottish engineer, Fleeming Jenkin. Jenkin pointed out that Darwin's *blended inheritance* model of reproduction, in which features of an organism would appear blended with features of its mate in their offspring, would not permit a salient feature, such as a new adaptation, to subsist. A single red dot in a population of gray dots would not produce more red dots, but a series of half-red dots that would gradually recede into indistinction. Darwin was startled by this criticism and began to emphasize that variation must exist across a population (many red dots at once, and consistently more successful than their rivals) for it to take root (Beatty 2010, 29). But the more compelling solution came with the Modern Evolutionary Synthesis, which drew on the discovery of the gene to postulate the theory of *particulate inheritance*: rather than *blending* features, the gene reserves a structural integrity that is passed down, reasserting itself as a particular feature in later generations even if it is only present in trace amounts – as when two brown-eyed parents have a blue-eyed child. This allows much more flexibility in the production of breeding populations with sufficient reservoirs of a phenotype-level feature for it to emerge as dominant.

The EES framework applies this same framework to what is called the *evolution of evolvability*, which means the extent to which organisms are more or less able to change over the course of successive generations in response to contingencies in their environments (Wagner & Draghi 2010, 380). This, too, is a mechanical process, relating to greater or lesser degrees of flexibility in the expression of genes. The concept is developed, in part, by pointing to all the organisms that *no longer exist* because they were *not evolvable enough* – or too evolvable. Too little evolvability leaves an organism susceptible to disaster when its environment changes around it. But too much evolvability can also be a liability if it drains an organism's energy and resources to maintain flexibility in a static environment where more narrowly focused competitors or predators can run the tables.

What all of these insights point to is that evolution is a resolutely *physical* process – a process that is only possible because of a concrete dynamic of conservation *and* variation, structure *and* change. To elevate one of these components over the other, as Massumi does, following Bergson, makes no sense. Genetic transformation is not a function of the "power of expressive mentality," any more than wind and rain eroding a rock formation are expressive mentality. What evolution looks like under the microscope is a crisp, if massively complex, material process, a sort of bricolage in which existing fixed forms are assembled and recombined in new ways. Bricolage without a supply of forms to draw on would be empty, just as the forms without dynamism would be an endless repetition of the same.

The Intransigence of Power

This misunderstanding of the relationship between affects and organisms leads to the problems with Massumi's rendition of the analytics of power. One of the main features of Foucault's analytics of power is that power is "a multiple and mobile field of force relations" (Foucault 1990, 102). Rather than being unified, Foucault sees power as operating through multiple channels. Rather than being a unidirectional application of force, it is a set of "force relations." The task of an analytics of power must be to develop tools for tracking these attributes.

Massumi's version of power falls short of this in several ways. His theory of Ronald Reagan's successful marshalling of becoming is one example. It suggests that power works to the extent that it is able to channel fluctuation – to harness becoming. This echoes the romantic streak in Deleuze in which animality is located as a sort of emancipatory force: "we are able to surpass the given," Massumi writes, "to the exact degree to which we assume our instinctive animality" (Massumi 2014, 38). But for Foucault, power is a situation we are always invested in, even when we resist. The most sustained operations of power, for Foucault, are disciplinary practices – the "political technologies of the body," often repetitive, always yielding durable effects – which are required for resistance no less than they are required for oppression. "The body," he writes, "becomes a useful force only if it is both a productive body and a subjected body" (Foucault 1975, 26). Hence Foucault insists that liberation movements need an "ethics" – a set of disciplinary practices studiously applied to the self (Foucault 1984, 343 and see the section "Economies of Dignity: Reconsidering the Mosque Movement"). It's hard to square this with a vocabulary of becoming.

This is the line of thought that prompts William Mazzarella's concern about the Deleuzian dialect of affect theory – that it "bequeathed to the philosophies it spawned a crudely romantic distinction between, on the one side, all-encompassing form (whose totalizing ambition must be resisted) and, on the other side, the evanescent forms of affective and – it is often implied – popular potentiality (which must be nurtured and celebrated)" (Mazzarella 2009, 301). As Foucault insists, "there is no locus of great Refusal, no soul of revolt, source of all rebellions, or pure law of the revolutionary" (Foucault 1990, 96). Becoming may be a workable model of the play of substance within the field of difference and repetition. But this is exactly what makes affect-as-becoming an unhelpful way of thinking about power.

The most pointed criticism of Deleuzian affect theory, however, comes from within affect theory itself, in Eve Sedgwick and Adam Frank's 1995 essay "Shame in the Cybernetic Fold." Here, they write that the approach that liquidates all response to a single stream of affect is

> like a scanner or copier that can reproduce any work of art in 256,000 shades of gray. However infinitesimally subtle its discriminations may be, there are crucial knowledges it simply cannot transmit unless it is equipped to deal with the coarsely reductive possibility that red is different from yellow is different again from blue. (Sedgwick 2003, 114)

The model of politics as becoming limits the analytics of power by reducing power to just one thing, one particular affective template: *enthusiasm*. In this dialect, politics can be *affective* or *non-affective* – a choice is made by political actors to employ or to shun an *affective strategy*. But this makes no sense from a Foucauldian perspective. For Foucault, the field of power relations is multiple, but not binary. Just as Elspeth Probyn insists there can be no affectless writing, a Foucauldian approach suggests there can be no affectless politics (Probyn 2005).

As Eugenie Brinkema points out: "In the end, ethics, politics, aesthetics – indeed, lives – must be enacted in the definite particular" (Brinkema 2014, xv). The Deleuzian sense of affect can't capture the real multiplicity of affects, the way that power is channeled through the interplay of specific embodied forms rather than the "pure plastic rhythm" of becoming (Manning 2009, 6). Rather than an animal politics, it is a politics of radio static. Just as the grad student at the conference probably started out, like me, mildly buzzed by the art installation, she was eventually driven to drink. If *affect* in the sense of becoming were tantamount to power, then we'd be irresistibly pulled to it like moths fluttering to a lamp. When an animal body is enfolded in a zone of pure becoming, that body is not attracted, but feels itself unraveling.

In a review of a recent book on Deleuze, Greg Seigworth writes that "the privileging of a proto-materialist/sensationalist Deleuze, especially for more than a few who have written in the wake of Brian Massumi's influential *Parables for the Virtual*, has led to a sometimes rather reductive reading ... of Deleuze's affectual ontology" (Seigworth 2007, 3–4). Seigworth is pushing back on a tendency to overweight what we might identify as the Bergsonian strands of Deleuze's thought – the emphasis on *differences in kind* – rather than the monist, materialist, and Spinozist strands. Versions of affect theory that resolutely swing affect into the column of the virtual, becoming, and the excessive are an expression, I would argue, of this tendency to resolve a tension within Deleuze's own thought decisively in favor of Bergsonism. Whereas Deleuze's rhizome is a carefully calibrated image of the dynamic between becoming and concrescence, between lines of flight and tubers, the amplification of the Bergsonian tone obliterates this attention to materiality, producing a chain of synonyms for *becoming* that dangerously depart from a meaningful theory of power.

"Why not walk on your head, sing with your sinuses, see through your skin, breathe with your belly?" Deleuze and Guattari ask with a gleam in their eye in *A Thousand Plateaus* (Deleuze & Guattari 1987, 151). This reflects the dream of a certain understanding of affect as pure potentiality, as a field of total becoming. What it misses is the material dynamic of enablement and constraint that is the condition of embodied life – of all life. Organisms require *organization*. To exist, they must programmatically limit the openness of matter through a process of biological structuring. This is why, Monique Scheer observes, for all the capacity of history and culture to sequence bodies in novel ways, "no human society will develop a dance step that requires five feet or a musical instrument made for a hand with eight digits" (Scheer 2012, 201). Understanding how bodies converge into broader social systems requires an understanding of embodiment in its specificity. As Mazzarella writes, "For all its claims to enable a new, radical form of socio-cultural analysis, such a standpoint in practice prevents us from understanding the workings of any actually existing social institutions, because it has always already dismissed their mediating practices as having compromised the potentialities that a more *im-mediate* vitality would embody" (Mazzarella 2009, 302). The genre of paeans to transformation indulged in by Deleuze is a romantic residue, presuming that the constant fluctuation of becoming at the level of substance is relevant at the level of politics. Its contribution to a theory of power is limited at best.

3 The Animality of Affect

To track the multiple textures of politics, we need to engage with versions of affect that deal with its animality, rather than its autonomy. There are a number of avenues for doing this. This section explores dialects of affect theory that point us back to affect in its embodied, material specificity to create a better platform for affect theory to engage with the analytics of power. Two specific articulations of affect theory will be explored to this end: Eve Sedgwick's encounter with Silvan Tomkins and Sara Ahmed's dialogue with phenomenology. Rather than simply abandoning the Deleuzian dialect, however, these frameworks offer, I will argue, a new avenue for incorporating the concept of *becoming* by including it as a particular affective configuration corresponding to the phenomenology of novelty. At the same time, this section will consider criticisms of these approaches, especially Ruth Leys's sustained attack on Tomkins.

The Tomkins Dialect: Affect Foundationalism

One set of cues for framing affect theory according to the coordinates of animality comes from the twentieth-century psychologist Silvan Tomkins, particularly in the reading of his work offered by Eve Kosofsky Sedgwick. Tomkins is explicit about his debt to Darwin, and especially to Darwin's late work *The Expression of the Emotions in Man and Animals*. Janet Browne has argued that Darwin's project after the publication of *Origin of Species* in 1859 was to add as much supplemental material to his original theory as possible. As part of this priority, Darwin became increasingly interested, throughout the 1860s, in facial expressions as a physiological feature that can be identified across humans and nonhuman mammals (Browne 2002, 304; Darwin 2009, 23). *Expression* was originally intended to be a section of Darwin's earlier *Descent of Man*, but the project mushroomed so quickly that Darwin found himself compelled to publish it as a separate book. The animality of affect for Darwin is the mark of our cognitive and emotive continuity with nonhuman animals.

Tomkins, a psychologist at Princeton who laid out alternatives to psychoanalytic and behaviorist models of emotion, operated in a lineage of psychologists of emotion that included not only Darwin, but William James and Sigmund Freud. Tomkins' approach, however, is difficult to pin down. Although he participated in the turn to modern experimental science and made some of his own experiments central to his defense of his views, he clearly bears the marks of his graduate training in philosophy, frequently writing more like a reflective humanist than a data-driven scientist. Moreover, his published work spans several decades, including, notoriously, his four-volume work *Affect Imagery Consciousness*, which saw the first two volumes published in the 1960s and the latter two almost thirty years later, during which time his own ideas – and the field around him – had transformed.

However, Tomkins' work can be summarized as a development of a few distinct but loosely interconnected ideas. One is the emphasis on a set of basic emotions which he, following Darwin, saw as evolved from animal ancestors.

Tomkins takes Darwin's *The Expression of the Emotions in Man and Animals* as a foundation for this project, but shifts the frame from a focus on *expression* to *motivation*. This shift allows him to craft Darwin's work into a counterpoint to the behaviorist paradigm of his time, which emphasized learned, conditioned responses and rejected appeals to internal states. This counterpoint came to be called the Basic Emotions hypothesis, a set of discrete emotional drivers embedded in brains (Tomkins 1981, 310).

Tomkins moved from a list of seven to a list of nine such basic emotions, starting with *Surprise-Startle, Distress-Anguish, Anger-Rage, Enjoyment-Joy, Interest-Excitement, Fear-Terror*, and *Shame-Humiliation*; later adding *Dissmell* and *Disgust*. Tomkins' premise was that humans did not evolve to be perfectly measured mechanisms, but organisms roughly and imperfectly fitted into their environments. This imperfect fit allowed for sophisticated dynamic responses – the ability to make errors and, in the case of more sophisticated animal organisms, to learn from them (Tomkins 2008, 8). "Modern evolutionary theory," Tomkins writes, "portrays man as an adapted organism, fearfully and wonderfully made, but also imperfectly adapted because he is a patchwork thrown together, bit by bit, without a plan, remodeled opportunistically as occasions permitted" (Tomkins 2008, 14).

Tomkins sees the affects as roughly jumbled-together components of this "magnificent makeshift" that is the human. Tomkins points out, as Darwin did in *The Origin of Species*, that emotional templates are heritable properties, as seen in traditions of animal husbandry that breed for particular dispositions (Tomkins 2008, 14; see also Darwin 1876, 211). Highly social animals – especially mammals, who fold a durable nurturance relationship between mother and offspring into their reproductive strategy – need to develop a deep repertoire of emotions to navigate the social interactions necessary for their survival and successful reproduction. These include, for Tomkins, "such characteristics as sensitivity to novel stimuli, sensitivity to social stimuli, aggressiveness, timidity and other affects" (Tomkins 2008, 14). This yields the distinctive affective landscape of human bodies, our many peaks and valleys – but Tomkins is careful to emphasize that our main encounter with affects is always as an alloy. An affect, he suggests, is "like a letter of an alphabet in a language, changing in significance as it is assembled with varying other letters to form different words, sentences, paragraphs" (Tomkins 1981, 321).

This leads back to Tomkins' understanding of motivations. Here, he primarily differentiated himself from the reading of Freud prevalent in his intellectual moment, which identified the drive system as the origin of motivation. Drives, Tomkins observed, were motivations with rigidly fixed objects. The drives impelled bodies to go out into the world and find specific things to satisfy them – primarily food and sex. These drives then became the foundation for all other forms of motivation through sublimation. The energy of drives was diverted into other activities and interests.

Tomkins was dissatisfied with several aspects of this picture of motivation. For one thing, he noted that drives tended to be fungible, not "imperious." "Freud's id," he notes, "suddenly appeared to be a paper tiger since sexuality, as he best knew, was the most finicky of drives, easily rendered impotent by shame or anxiety or boredom or rage" (Tomkins 1981, 309). Why would the sex drive, this easily diverted thing, be sufficient to power so many other fascinations? This led into Tomkins' rejection of the "doctrine of sublimation" (Tomkins 1995, 49). Sublimation, he proposes, is useful for thinking about the limited relationship between sexuality and aggression, but its overbroad application to all sorts of passions and ambitions is unsustainable: "Activities as remote from sexuality as writing love poetry are not substitutes for sexuality per se," he writes, "Nor should they have been called instances of sublimation. Strictly speaking, what is involved is substitution of a symbolic object of love for a flesh and blood object of love, and love is primarily an affective phenomenon" (Tomkins 1995, 60).

It was the affect system that emerged for Tomkins as the motivational relay network that fuels all cognition and action. Drives were only successful, Tomkins argued, to the extent that they were able to mobilize the affect system. But the affect system was the more fundamental structure – a position we might call *affect foundationalism*.[8] "Without affect amplification nothing else matters," Tomkins quipped, "and with its amplification anything can matter" (Tomkins 1981, 322). This is why the sex drive could be so easily diverted or even outright defeated: its heavy reliance on the affective arousal system left it susceptible to redirection. "Sublimation" is but one mode of the process of affective redirection, not the type case of an overarching process by which "drive energy" is redirected.

Tomkins's proposal was that the affect system needed to be understood as the very substance of reward, value, and motivation itself. He identified affect as "the bottom line for thought as well as perception and behavior .... Affect is an end in itself, with or without instrumental behavior" (Tomkins 1981, 321). Rather than seeing affect as the garnish of action – a fringe benefit – which was itself directed by sovereign reason, Tomkins located it as the churning center of gravity of the matrix out of which all decisions issue. By dictating what matters, the affect system is the only thing that can make bodies move.

---

[8] My thanks to David Decosimo for suggesting this term to me.

Tomkins' argument for shifting the framing in this way was built in part out of a complex engagement with cybernetics theory, an attempt to explicate the elemental components required to make a more-or-less free organism. But it was also sourced in a consideration of Darwinian themes – not only human continuity with animals, but the line of continuity from infants to adult humans. Like Darwin, Tomkins found inspiration in watching his newborn children, leading to his organized rejection of what he saw as a *cognitivist* orthodoxy in psychology. "There are today a majority of theorists," he wrote,

> who postulate an evaluating, appraising homunculus (or at the least, an appraising process) that scrutinizes the world and declares it as an appropriate candidate for good or bad feelings. Once information has been so validated, it is ready to activate a specific affect. Such theorists, like Everyman, cannot imagine feeling without an adequate "reason." (Tomkins 1981, 316)

But Tomkins argued that such a *reason-first* theory made no sense when applied to infants. It leads to the impression of "a foetus in its passage down the birth canal collecting its thoughts, and upon being born emitting a birth cry after having appraised the extrauterine world as a vale of tears" (Tomkins 1981, 316). Tomkins began, then, with a sensing body, a bunched net of affects driving responses. Out of this net gradually emerge more sophisticated contraptions of affect, some of which looked like not-affect – like sovereign reason itself. This placed humans and animals on a long plane of continuity, a sprawling menagerie of organisms foundationally defined by their affective pulses.

As animal studies scholar Kari Weil has written, the turn to animals is a way of responding to a certain frustration with the acute emphasis on language in poststructualist accounts of knowledge and experience – "an attempt not only to escape from post-structuralism's linguistic trap but to reexamine its confines" (Weil 2012, 12). The affective turn and the animal turn can be almost exactly mapped onto each other, efficiently reducing the number of turns in the humanities by one. The animality of affect, then, is a framework that emphasizes the evolved elements of emotion, while also placing those elements into a configurable matrix that illuminates how they can be arranged into distinct configurations through the frames of culture, history, and biography. It offers a picture of humans and other animals as what New Materialist theorist Samantha Frost would call *biocultural cultures* (Frost 2016).

The relationship between these two facets of Tomkins' thought – basic emotions and affect as raw motivation – is deep, but they can be meaningfully disaggregated from one another. Sedgwick's investigation of Tomkins, often in collaboration with her colleague Adam Frank, brings up the basic emotions hypothesis to redraw the slant of contemporary theory, and uses affect foundationalism to reframe queer culture and sexuality. In the introductory chapter to *Shame and Its Sisters*, Sedgwick and Frank propose that theory in the humanities has drifted into a reflexive anti-essentialist posture that is itself a form of essentialism. They argue that it's not so easy to walk away from a model of, for instance, human subjectivity: even a radically constructivist position is, ultimately, an ontology of human beings as *essentially* plastic and uniformly susceptible to influences in their environment, a position with its own well-fortified position in the lineage of western philosophical idealism. "There is not a choice waiting to be made, in evaluating theoretical models," they argue, "between essentialism and no essentialism. If there's a choice it is between differently structured residual essentialisms" (Sedgwick 2003, 114).

Sedgwick and Frank use this framework to differentiate their version of affect from the Deleuzian dialect, which they locate as an offshoot of the radical anti-biologism of contemporary theory. They convert Tomkins' approach into a formula: *finitely many, $n > 2$* (Sedgwick 2003, 108). It means that affect is not singular, nor is it binary, nor is it infinite. Rather than a single stream of affect that can be turned on or off, affect is a multiplicity that runs through every aspect of human experience. But it is also *finitely multiple*. Rather than an abstract infinitude (which returns to a binary of finite/infinite), it manifests as a bricolage of available forms, the product of an evolutionarily particular bio-architecture.

Sedgwick and Frank are not especially interested in the particulars of Tomkins' affect inventory. (Tomkins, too, spent little time defending his nine-point diagram, so this may not be any kind of betrayal.) They find in Tomkins a way to displace what they see as a stiflingly rigid anti-essentialist orthodoxy settling over "what theory knows today":

> we fear, with the installation of an *automatic* anti-biologism as the unshifting central tenet of 'theory,' the loss of conceptual access to an entire thought realm, the analogic realm of finitely many (n>2) values. Access to this realm is important for, among other things, enabling a political vision of difference that might resist both binary homogenization and infinitizing trivialization. (Sedgwick 2003, 108)

Crucially, though, they pursue Tomkins precisely because the biological axis is, for him, so profoundly plastic. Tomkins' version of affect theory suggests that the biological is better understood not as fixed, but as compounding. The broad gamut of human behavior is a function of our high degree of cognitive flexibility in placing different things together. Affects for Tomkins, Sedgwick notes, "can be, and are, attached to things, people, ideas, sensations, relations, activities, ambitions, institutions, and any number of other things, including other affects"

(Sedgwick 2003, 19). This would seem to align with the approach proposed by historian of emotions William Reddy, who argues for a "formal theory that establishes emotions as largely (but not entirely) learned" (Reddy 2004, xi).

Sedgwick and Frank see this commitment to (finite) variability expressed in a literary device they identify within Tomkins' work, what they call the *if-may statement*. Tomkins, they note, has a tendency to write blocks of sentences constructed in parallel using the formula *If I . . . you may . . .* " (and the reverse; Sedgwick 2003, 100). Rather than a determinism, Tomkins offers a matrix for mapping the contingent connections between bodies and histories – the veins of affect animating our values. As Tomkins writes, "[t]he basic power of the affect system is a consequence of its freedom to combine with a variety of other components . . . " (Tomkins 1981, 324). This means that to know another is to know them in their intimate complexity = their own unique topography of values, desires, memories, and attachments = not as a deterministic caricature.

Moreover, Sedgwick finds in Tomkins's work a way of emphasizing affect's operation as an end in itself. She writes that "in contrast to the instrumentality of drives and their direct orientation toward an aim different from themselves, the affects can be autotelic" (Sedgwick 2003, 19). In other words, the *telos* – endpoint – of the affect, is the affect itself, not some goal beyond the affect. What we want *is* to feel. In her hands this becomes a roadmap to a more acute attention to embodiment, sensation, and feeling as the substance of subjectivity.

However, when Tomkins relegates affect to a binary of positive and negative, Sedgwick is eager to move on. Ever attentive to the need for a richer, lusher theory of queerness, Sedgwick suggests that we need to take Tomkins' extraordinary vortex of recombinant affects as ultimately overrunning the positive/negative binary itself. Her cardinal example of this is shame. Clearly a negative affect for Tomkins, Sedgwick rescripts shame as – at least sometimes – a resource. She makes shame an ineradicable feature of subjectivity, "a kind of free radical that . . . attaches to and permanently intensifies or alters the meaning of – almost anything: a zone of the body, a sensory system, a prohibited or indeed a permitted behavior . . ." (Sedgwick 2003, 62). Shame is liquid sensitivity. It can be acutely oppressive as well as a source of a kind of pleasure.

Sedgwick goes so far as to name this *queer performativity*: "a strategy for the production of meaning and being, in relation to the affect shame and to the later and related fact of stigma" (Sedgwick 2003, 61). This shame-running queer performativity furnishes the background coordinates out of which enriching and gorgeous pieces of culture are created, such as camp. Rather than understanding camp as parody, Sedgwick suggests it reflects a finely choreographed dalliance with shame that brings out extravagant joy, a "visceral, operatic power"

(Sedgwick 2011, 66). Camp is carefully congealed shame, a controlled fermentation that produces intoxicating effects. Tomkins' focus on affect as an end in itself lets Sedgwick redraw the map of queer aesthetics.

What's at stake for Sedgwick in this? She tells us in so many ways, but I suggest a clue comes in her earlier essay "How to Bring Your Kids up Gay." Sedgwick uses this article as a venue to challenge some psychoanalytic accounts of the emergence of queer desire, for instance, the claim made by some that "[t]he reason effeminate boys turn out gay . . . is that other men don't validate them as masculine" (Sedgwick 1993, 159). She points out that a radically constructivist idiom for conceptualizing sexuality – even where impelled by seemingly progressive motives – leads to a recipe for queerness and, conversely, a recipe for its eradication, "the overarching, hygienic Western fantasy of a world without any more homosexuals in it" (Sedgwick 1993, 163). She's exasperated, but also frightened, by an insistence that desire is nothing more than a layering of childhood experiences that abandon the specificity of bodies. "People are different from each other," she asserts as her first axiom in *Epistemology of the Closet*, before continuing, in a line that more than any other offers a premonition of the dialect of affect theory she would create: "It is astonishing how few respectable conceptual tools we have for dealing with this self-evident fact" (Sedgwick 1990, 22).

Sedgwick's take on Tomkins, then, is that he is a far better touchstone for theoretical reflection for the humanities – especially in sexuality studies – than Freud (Sedgwick 2003, 120). He does this precisely by reiterating our animality – by emphasizing the felt life of desire, power, and thought, in congress with language, but phylogenetically prior to it.

The Critique of Basic Emotions Theory

It's important to mention that the Basic Emotions hypothesis is highly contested within the field of psychology of emotions. Lisa Feldman Barrett, for instance, offers a sustained, book-length argument against what she characterizes as the *classical view of emotions*, which includes the idea that emotions are "distinct, recognizable phenomena inside us" (Barrett 2017, x). Barrett's main line of argument is that direct evidence of basic emotions – such as sadness or fear – across cultures is scarce; experiments that seem to furnish evidence for the existence of basic emotions across cultures are tainted by poorly designed experiments or by working with cultures that have already been saturated by western preconceptions about emotional expression (Barrett 2017, 53). Her primary target is the research of Paul Ekman, a student of Tomkins whose work focused on the universality of facial expressions. Although Ekman takes the brunt of her criticism, Tomkins' Basic Emotions paradigm is in the blast zone (Barrett 2017, 7). Her alternative proposal is that rather than emotions as such, we have a set of *emotion categories*, best understood on the analogy with populations making up a species (Barrett 2017, 24).

The question prompted by Barrett's line of criticism, for our purposes, is whether the ambiguous status of the Basic Emotions hypothesis pushes us to settle on the Deleuzian understanding of affect. As Barrett writes,

> Affect is the general sense of feeling that you experience throughout each day. It is not emotion but a much simpler feeling with two features. The first is how pleasant or unpleasant you feel, which scientists call *valence*. The pleasant-ness of the sun on your skin, the deliciousness of your favorite food, and the discomfort of a stomachache or a pinch are all examples of affective valence. The second feature of affect is how calm or agitated you feel, which is called *arousal*. (Barrett 2017, 72)

But the affect-emotion distinction used by Barrett is not at all like Massumi's, in that she sees affects and emotions as zones on a continuum, rather than different in kind. Affects are the micro region of feeling (and they can be felt); emotions are conglomerates of these pulses scaled up to the register of overwhelming awareness.

The second point to be made is that a contested scientific thesis is not necessarily wrong. Scientific hypotheses always go through a period of con-testation before they become settled science – and even then they can be reopened to controversy. The debate surrounding the status of emotions as basic or constructed is a live scientific conversation. For this reason, it would be reckless of humanists to compel any one interpretation to do too much load-bearing work. But the questions that are urgent and interesting to scientists are not necessarily vital to humanists. The humanities don't operate at the level of precision of, for instance, enumerating a fixed, concrete repertoire of transcul-tural human emotion templates, just as the sciences would be hamstrung if they set out to explore the nexus of bodies and power armed solely with data from laboratory experiments.

My suggestion is that humanists can wade into discussions about Basic Emotions if they so choose – exploring how certain emotional categories appear or recede across times and places – but can also stay agnostic about its overall viability. This agnostic position doesn't require abandoning emotion-words as analytical tools: humanists don't need to have a firm set of commitments about whether *happiness* or *fear* is deep-seated natural kinds in order to build a meaningful analysis of sadness or fear. Moreover, as Jan Plamper points out, humanists can offer indispensable framing to scientific research by helping to contextualize the outputs of laboratory work: "If neuroscientists carry out a brain scan they will need to take greater account of the fact that they are not scanning 'the brain', but are scanning one individual brain, one with an individual biography, belonging to a particular group, from a particular culture, at a particular time" (Plamper 2015, 248).[9]

Tomkins and Intentionalism

A more sustained broadside against Tomkins is found in Leys' *The Ascent of Affect*, alongside her attack on Massumi. Ekman is Leys' primary target, but she also extends her criticisms to Tomkins and Sedgwick herself. The section "Unbecoming: Criticisms of the Deleuzian Dialect of Affect Theory" looked at the advantages and liabilities of Leys' critique of Massumi. One of the central projects of Leys' work is drawing a parallel between Tomkins-influenced affect theorists and Deleuze-influenced affect theorists.[10] Tomkins' commitment to basic emotions would seem to be fundamentally incompatible with Massumi's emphasis on affects as pre-personal and therefore prior to emotions. But unlike Barrett, Leys is not primarily concerned with the basic emotions problem. She sees a deeper continuity uniting the compendium of thinkers working on affect: the theme of *anti-intentionalism* – their opposition to the intentionalist view "that emotions are directed at cognitively apprehended objects and are sensitive to 'reasons'" (Leys 2017, 4). The tactical necessity for her is to show that all of these thinkers are committed to a theory of affects as sharply separated from cognitive objects, and that, therefore, Tomkins, Ekman, and Sedgwick are conceptually isomorphic with Deleuze and Massumi.

Leys reads Tomkins as a radically anti-intentionalist thinker, one who "argued that the affects and cognition constituted two entirely separate systems, and that accordingly the emotions should be theorized in anti-intentionalist terms" (Leys 2017, 19). She takes Tomkins' suggestion that the affect system has an overriding priority in dictating motivation as proof of his belief in a fissure between cognition and affect. The upshot of all this, for Leys, is that Tomkins's theory

> makes it a delusion to say you are happy because your child got a job, or sad because your mother died, for the simple reason that your child's getting a job, or your mother's death, is only a trigger for your happiness or sadness, emotions that could in principle be triggered by something else. In other words, Tomkins held that the affects are inherently objectless, because they

---

[9] I discuss avenues of interaction between the humanities and the sciences further in the Conclusion.

[10] This continues Leys' debate with the affect theorists who responded to her initial article in the pages of *Critical Inquiry* (see Connolly 2011, 792; Frank & Wilson 2012, 870).

are bodily responses, like a sneeze or an orgasm or an itch: I laugh when I am
tickled, but I am not laughing at you (at anything). (Leys 2017, 33)

Leys reads Tomkins as, in other words, essentially advancing a version of the
affects no different from the spectral dualist rendition of Deleuze, which locates
affect on a register that is different in kind from cognition.

There are several questionable features of Leys' awkward, straightjacketed
interpretation – an interpretation very few scholars who take cues from Tomkins
would recognize. Most thinkers who reference Tomkins see in him a resource
for trying to chart the dynamic webbing *linking* cognition and feeling. Tomkins'
student Donald S. Nathanson writes in the preface to *Affect Imagery
Consciousness* that, when asked why there were no commas in the title,
Tomkins responded "Because there isn't any way to separate the three interlocked concepts" (Nathanson 2008, xi). Tomkins' relevance for experimental
psychology may well have waned, but his relevance in his philosophical mode
for a different set of questions and concerns in the humanities would seem to
still be bright. My sense is that there is a pattern of errors in Leys' reading of
Tomkins, hence I'll present excerpts from her writing here at length.

Take the passage Leys places as the epigraph to her chapter on Tomkins:
"Cognition without affect is weak; affect without cognition is blind" (in Leys
2017, 27). There is an interpretation available that Tomkins is proposing an
acute split between affect and cognition here, but I think most readers would
sense that Tomkins is writing about a dynamic, not a binary. This becomes
clearer when one studies the passage in context.

> The human being is the most complex system in nature; his superiority over
> other animals is as much a consequence of his more complex affect system as
> it is of his more complex analytical capacities. Out of the marriage of reason
> with affect there issues clarity with passion. Reason without affect would be
> impotent, affect without reason would be blind. The combination of affect
> and reason guarantees man's high degree of freedom. (Tomkins 2008, 63)

Tomkins is describing how organisms navigate ambiguous environments by
learning about them. This trajectory of learning requires a certain degree of
openness to risk and ambiguity. In contrast to the drive model of psychoanalysis, in which we navigate the world by responding in fixed ways to
specific objects, the affect system offers a nuanced mechanism for recalibrat-
ing our responses by tinkering with our net of motivations and attachments.
Tomkins sees this as *fundamentally* affective, but the claim that this leaves us
in a state in which affects are radically *divorced* from reason does not follow.
To add to her brief against him, Leys quotes Tomkins as saying, "*We distin-
guish sharply the cause of an affect from its object. We will argue that every*

affect arousal has one or more causes but that it may or may not have an object" (in Leys 2017, 40ff, Leys' emphasis). But Tomkins is not saying affects are *intrinsically* divorced from objects, only that there is no *necessary* relationship between them – the crucial difference between *cannot be* and *might not be*.

Leys writes that for Tomkins, "free-floating distress or anxiety of the kind one might attribute to the wailing infant is a paradigm of the affects just because it is free floating and hence can be experienced without relation to an object or to cognition. Although we may search to provide the anxiety with an object, there is no object to which it inherently belongs" (Leys 2017, 34). But now we see a confusion of *doesn't inherently belong* with *cannot belong*. Certainly, Tomkins wants to say that there are only a handful of instances where an affect is more or less insolubly attached to a particular object – all of them mapping closely onto the Freudian template of "drives." But Tomkins is not arguing that a noninherent relationship is a non-relationship. He's proposing that the high latitude of cognitive plasticity of humans and some other large-brained animals means motivational force *can be* attached to a range of different things: "Although affects which are activated by drives and by special releasers have a limited range of objects, the linkage of affects to objects through thinking enormously extends the range of the objects of positive and negative feeling," he writes, before continuing: "There is literally no kind of object which has not historically been linked to one or another of the affects" (Tomkins 1995, 54). It's a mistake to say Tomkins thinks there *can't* be a meaningful association between an affect and an object in mind. His point is that there is a dizzying variety of possible associations. The infant wailing because she's cold or hungry or lonely isn't so much the *paradigm* as the seed of the sophisticated affective subject that the infant matures into.

Leys tends to conceptualize Tomkins as a politically normative thinker, rather than a diagnostic one. She writes that "according to such theorists [as Tomkins and Massumi] . . . affect has the potential to transform individuals for good or ill without regard to the content of argument or debate" (Leys 2017, 323). She goes on to infer that "since Tomkins defined ideology as 'any organized set of ideas about which human beings are at once most articulate and most passionate, and for which there is no evidence and about which they are least certain,' it appears he thought our ideas and beliefs cannot be defended by good arguments because they are not rational but nonrational, nonintentional affective phenomena" (Leys 2017, 48). And she disdains his belief that "an understanding of the putative emotional experiences that lead people to hold the beliefs they do can stand in for an independent assessment of the truth or falsity of those same beliefs" (Leys 2017, 47).

Leys writes that for Tomkins, "although the affects may be activated by reasons, this is only because they have been coassembled with the separate cognitive system. In themselves they lack rationality, which is to say that their functions do not belong to what the American philosopher Wilfred Sellars (1912–1989) called the 'logical space of reasons'" (Leys 2017, 43). This is half-true. Affects lack *reason* in the sense that you can't necessarily sit down and explain them. They bring their own agency to the table, which means they aren't waiting for "reason" to tell them what to do. It means they can push their own agenda, not that they are outside of causes. It means you might get in a fight with your spouse because you're off-kilter after being abused by your boss. Or you might start crying over a TV commercial because you only got 4 hours of sleep.

Leys's line of attack is to invoke outrage at Tomkins' willingness to throw over critique in favor of a picture of how "psychobiographical origins" shape belief (Leys 2017, 47). Here, she misses that Tomkins is naming a state of affairs, not celebrating it. (Who would claim that beliefs aren't shaped by psychobiography?) Does he think beliefs can't be dislodged through dialog? That seems farfetched, especially if one considers that his definition of *ideology* is almost certainly not to be taken as a generalized definition of *belief*.[11] *Ideology* is a set of belief-attachments that are cued up by a subject's material circumstances and so are especially immune to critique. Tomkins' insight is to identify this immunity as a function of affect and, in the process, provide an exceptionally deft explanation for how rival immunized information spheres have become the dominant feature of our current public landscape. Leys assumes Tomkins is undermining truth value for sport, rather than offering a deep account of how we arrive at our assessments of truthfulness.

No conventional reader of Tomkins thinks that the emphasis in Tomkins' work is on the radical incongruence of affects and objects, certainly not Sedgwick, who writes that she was drawn to Tomkins precisely because of his supple account of the nexus of experience, feeling, thought, and subjectivity – and in particular the way this subtle account of the simultaneous delicacy and binding force of affects leaves the "heterosexist teleology" of psychoanalysis askew (Sedgwick 2003, 99). The versatility of the affect system maps onto what Sedgwick sees as an imperative within the humanities to track subjectivity in its locality and specificity, as complex layerings of biological, personal, historical, and cultural attachments to the objects that make up a living world. So too, with Probyn, who writes that "In shame, the feeling and minding and thinking and social body comes alive" (Probyn 2005, 34–5). Her textured, thoughtful account

---

[11] This becomes even more plausible when we add in an account of the affective dimension of good or true knowledge, including scientific knowledge. See Schaefer (2017).

of the shame of living as a white body in a settler society like Australia would make no sense if the hinge between feeling and cognition had been shattered (Probyn 2005, 100).

Ultimately, I can't square Leys' reading of Tomkins as stipulating a rigid divide between affect and cognition with statements like this one:

> The interrelationships between the affect of interest and the functions of thought and memory are so extensive that absence of the affective support of interest would jeopardize intellectual development no less than destruction of brain tissue. To think, as to engage in any other human activity, one must care, one must be excited, must be continually rewarded. There is no human competence which can be achieved in the absence of a sustaining interest, and the development of cognitive competence is peculiarly vulnerable to anomie. (Tomkins 1995, 76–7)

There may be psychologists who read Tomkins as a devout anti-intentionalist, but the consideration of Tomkins in the humanities has not, to my knowledge, fallen along these lines.

On the first page of her book Leys expresses what sounds like annoyance with emotion science: "The impression left is of a scientific domain in stasis, one in which the majority of researchers cling to their contested positions and research strategies, leaving fundamental questions unresolved" (Leys 2017, 1). It may be stasis, or it may be a slow-moving scientific conversation in which different sides are continuing to gather data, develop interpretations, and explore zones of compromise. Leys seems distressed that there is no consensus. But is consensus a reasonable demand of a hyper-complicated scientific field like the brain-mind sciences in which techniques of measurement and the parameters of the objects under study are all moving targets? Science doesn't work by moving from consensus to consensus. It works by opening realms of dissensus and allowing consensus to emerge from a long, halting, and noisy process of exploration. The claim that the natural resting state of science is consensus resembles the discredited logical positivist view of science, in which a theory is logically inferred from a given data set and only expanded as our data set improves. To say "There is no consensus – science must not be working" is to fundamentally misunderstand the nature of scientific discovery.

In a series of responses and counter-responses in *Critical Inquiry* in the early 2010s, Leys wrote "It is precisely because I appreciate science that I draw the line at bad science" (Leys 2011, 803). No doubt, there has been significant pushback on Ekman, and a near-total repudiation of the Libet experiments documenting the "missing half-second." But beyond this, Leys is walking into swampy territory, presenting her work as a genealogy of a scientific conversation that is, in fact, designed to present to humanities scholars a decisively resolved interpretation of an open field of scientific questions.

Leys, as a trauma theorist, is perhaps wary of depleting the agency of traumatized subjects, and so sees it as necessary to reassert the image of a sovereign self, an "intact person," that is in full command and full awareness of their own horizon of being. The commingled nexus sticking together affects, cognition, and objects *is* a problem for Tomkins – and a problem that he doubtless responds to in somewhat different ways at different moments in his long career. Arguably, elaborating the complexity of that problem is the essence of his project and the reason why he has turned up as a resource for the theoretical humanities now. That's why it's shocking to attribute such a simplistic rule of affect/reason binarism to his thought. One query would be whether Leys could employ a hermeneutic of generosity with Tomkins, and perhaps find in him a more sympathetic resource.

All of this is to say that the Tomkins presented in Leys' pages is almost unrecognizable – certainly in the engagement of his thought by scholars such as Probyn and Sedgwick. His thinking is depicted as narrow, haughty, and rigid. Leys's insistence that all affect theorists can be slotted in the same anti-intentionalist container is based on her sense that they all allow affect a determinative role in shaping meaning. But this takes very different forms depending on whether the emphasis is placed on the autonomy of affect or the animality of affect – whether affect is located in a realm apart or seen as the inextricable property of a sprawling, shape-shifting system of cognition, intention, and subjectivity. There is merit to some of Leys' criticisms of Massumi, but the effort to lump Massumi and Tomkins together ultimately fails.

The Phenomenological Dialect: Impressionable Bodies

The animality of affect theory has been explored further through a dialect that takes cues from the field of phenomenology. The anthropologist Christopher Tilley offers a working definition of phenomenology as an approach emphasizing "the understanding and description of things as they are experienced by a subject" (Tilley 1994, 12). In the phenomenological vision, he adds "[t]he world and the subject reflect and flow into each other through the body that provides the living bond with the world" (Tilley 1994, 14). Phenomenology, then, like affect theory, centralizes concern with the felt life of a body moving through the world.[12] "If texture and affect," Sedgwick writes, "touching and feeling seem to belong together, then, it is not because they share a particular

---

[12] The phenomenological dialect in affect theory certainly merits its own volume for discussion. I will engage with it here as it intersects with the Tomkins dialect.

delicacy of scale, such as would necessarily call for 'close reading' or 'thick description.' What they have in common is that *at whatever scale they are attended to*, both are irreducibly phenomenological" (Sedgwick 2003, 21, emphasis original). The experiencing body serves as the focal concern for both phenomenology and affect theory. In the background here we can make out a genealogy connecting continental European philosophers such as Kant, Hegel, and Nietzsche to twentieth-century thinkers such as William James, Edmund Husserl, Martin Heidegger, and then the progenitors of affect theory such as Tomkins (who was inspired by James and described himself as a neo-Kantian (see: Nathanson 2008, xii)) and Gilles Deleuze – not to mention the hub role of a figure like Darwin linking Nietzsche and Tomkins.

At the forefront of the conversation linking phenomenology to affect theory is Sara Ahmed. Ahmed's 2006 book *Queer Phenomenology* contains her most precise articulation of this method: phenomenology, she writes, "can offer a resource for queer studies insofar as it emphasizes the importance of lived experience, the intentionality of consciousness, the significance of nearness or what is ready-to-hand, and the role of repeated and habitual actions in shaping bodies and worlds" (Ahmed 2006, 1). In her earlier work, Ahmed described how the accumulation of impressions from objects in the world shapes the horizon of feeling. The perimeter of the self is not the horizon of agency, but the bricolage of emotional textures that have imprinted themselves on our bodies. "*We need to remember the 'press' in an impression,*" she writes. "It allows us to associate the experience of having an emotion with the very affect of one surface upon another, an affect that leaves its mark or trace. So not only do I have an impression of others, but they also leave me with an impression; they impress me, and impress upon me" (Ahmed 2004c, 6, emphasis original). The horizon of our experience, she suggests, is itself made by the impressions left by the sprawling ensemble of interactions trailing our bodies.

Although Ahmed herself never, to my knowledge, makes this connection, the phenomenological tradition is closely correlated to a set of questions about animality. Part of the imperative of phenomenology as a project was to locate the accumulation of knowledge in experience rather than as a metaphysical property of intellect. Whereas intellect was implicitly or explicitly human, Edmund Husserl, the early twentieth-century founder of phenomenology, indicated that perception was a feature of animal minds no less than human minds: "the psyche or soul, the identical psychic being which, connected in a real way with the respective human or animal Body, makes up the substan-tial-real double being: the animal, man or brute" (Husserl 1987, 128). The set of phenomenological subjects of experience includes both human and animal bodies.

This inclusion of animals is fleshed out in the work of a figure who receives insufficient attention in affect theory, other than occasional mention in Elizabeth Grosz (1994) and Sara Ahmed (2006): the French phenomenologist Maurice Merleau-Ponty. Merleau-Ponty provided a vital correction to Husserl's core notion of the perceiving transcendental ego. He de-transcendentalized and de-egoized perception, locating the tissues of experience in the specific fleshy architecture of bodies. "[B]y thus remaking contact with the body and with the world," Merleau-Ponty writes, "we shall also rediscover ourself, since, perceiving as we do with our body, the body is a natural self and, as it were, the subject of perception" (Merleau-Ponty 1962, 239).

For Deleuze, phenomenology was anathema because it presupposed the integrity of the perceiving subject. But Merleau-Ponty and later phenomenologists, including Ahmed, saw the *subject* as something else. Rather than a crystalline unity, they found subjects to be bodies – each a sedimentation of forms and forces that enabled a historically particular mode of experience. The constituent parts of the body – contingent artifacts of slow-moving evolutionary histories – make up the instrumentation of perception. The erasure of these instruments does not leave us with a transcendental perceiving subject – the homunculus who had been peering through all those telescopes. It leaves us with nothing at all. No body, no plane of perception, no self. And the reconfiguration of the perceptual apparatus leaves us with a *different* self. In that sense, the subject of phenomenology is really a body, and a body is an assemblage of differently resonating material forms.

Merleau-Ponty expressly understands this in terms of animality, especially in his Darwin-influenced lectures on "Nature" and "The Structure of Behavior." Merleau-Ponty, following Jakob von Uexküll (like early Deleuze, as discussed in the section "The Deleuzian Dialect of Affect Theory"), suggests that animals experience the world in ways that correspond to a set of specific embodied priorities, shaped by both evolutionary lineages and individual learning (not to mention, we now know, epigenetic and ontogenetic factors) (von Uexküll 1957, 49). What we are left with is not a single faculty of perception, but a range of diverse animal bodies with different architectures of experience and sensation. These bio-architectures become the platforms of our affective encounters with the world. The kinds of animals we are make up the shape of how things feel to us. Each body has a repertoire of affective forms. We are returned to the necessity of an *ethological* approach, like that of the more Spinozist Deleuze: tracking animal bodies in their specificity. What Derrida called the "heterogeneous multiplicity" of animal bodies is an efflorescence of assemblages of affective avenues into the world, what I have elsewhere called ontophenomenologies (Derrida 2008, 31; see also Schaefer 2015).

Becoming and the Phenomenology of Novelty

Taken together, the Tomkins dialect and the phenomenological dialect provide an avenue for reframing affect in Deleuze's sense. Eugenie Brinkema writes that the Deleuzian sense of affect is synonymous with "resistance to systematicity, a promised recovery of contingency, surprise, play, pleasure, and possibility" (Brinkema 2014, 30). Rather than the core nature of affect, I would argue that this complex is *one affect among many*, a particular way of encountering the world that orients itself to the *experience of novelty*.

Deleuze's theory of novelty in his most Bergsonian moments is part of a long sequence of consonant terms in continental philosophy: Heidegger's German word *Ereignis* became the French *à venir* – that which is "to come" – and then the English *event*. In his final book with Guattari, *What Is Philosophy?*, Deleuze returns to the thematics of difference in kind, proposing that the true *concept* is the form of creation of something radically new on the terrain of thought (Deleuze & Guattari 1994, 18). "The concept speaks the event," they write, "not the essence or the thing – pure Event, a hecceity, an entity: the event of the Other or of the face (when, in turn, the face is taken as a concept)" (Deleuze & Guattari 1994, 21). Other thinkers such as Jacques Derrida and Alain Badiou play out a similar vocabulary, in which the event is a radical break from "what there is"[13] (Badiou 2001, 41; see also Malabou and Derrida 2004). In Massumi's work the event is associated with surplus, excess, and "life entering a new pulse of its own becoming" (Massumi 2014, 29).

For Deleuze in his more Bergsonian moments, the event is something we respond to because of its radical novelty – its trafficking in becoming. There's something intuitive about this proposition: we've all found ourselves swept up in moments of transformation and excitement. But as Mazzarella points out, this tips over into the language of romanticism and, ultimately, a form of abstraction. *Becoming* can be thrilling, but it can also be unwelcome, annoying, or exhausting. Moreover, the elevation of becoming to the essence of affect itself washes out our ability to talk about affects in their variety. In its more extreme forms, such as Badiou's event as the radically unforeseen, this language plummets into an abyss of abstraction. Somehow, for Badiou, every conversion experience is an affiliation to universalism. In an acute failure of imagination, the philosophy of the event tends to overlook the possibility that the encounter with radical novelty would yield something so profoundly unforeseen, so profoundly alien, that it would lead to the destruction of all forms of continuity with one's previous mode of being. In Badiou's book on St. Paul, for instance, it escapes

---

[13] The capacity to respond to this break is, at least for Badiou, that which "goes beyond the animal" (Badiou 2001, 41).

his notice that Paul on the road to Damascus trades one form of fanaticism for another (Badiou 2003). His conversion is more like getting a new wardrobe than a punctum of profound self-inversion.

How, then, to capture the insight of the Deleuzian dialect of affect theory – that power seems, not infrequently, to channel the exhilarating force of novelty – for a material analytics of power? My proposal is simply that the encounter with novelty must be, like all embodied productions, a structured, finite experience. Rather than an encounter with difference in kind, we as animal organisms have developed mechanisms for tracking a limited slice of the change, transformation, and novelty in the world. Rather than a radically transformative event, we are positioned by the *embodied phenomenology of novelty*.

From Tomkins' perspective, this corresponds to the affective spectrum of *interest-excitement*. As a continuum, the big emotion that we feel and call *excitement* is different in degree – but not in kind – from the microlevel affect which we also feel – but may or may not think to name – of *interest*. Interest is essentially responsive to "rate of change of information (which is within optimal limits)" (Tomkins 1995, 77). The Tomkins dialect of affect theory overlaps with the Deleuzian dialect to the extent that both are concerned with the affective currency of novelty. But Tomkins's tone diverges by emphasizing that the stimulation of this affective driver must be, in Nathanson's words, "both novel and safe" (Nathanson 2008, xvii). An excess of novelty overwhelms the body's finite appetite for interest, producing aversion and retreat. Rather than being different in kind, interest is a function of a body. Too little interest starves, but too much is toxic.

What the affective neuroscientist Jaak Panksepp calls the SEEKING system seems to correlate with this interest-excitement spectrum. Panksepp locates the origins of this system in evolution: a SEEKING system is an essential affective component for animal organisms as they become increasingly sophisticated and so increasingly specialized in the configuration of resources they need to survive and reproduce in their ecosystem. In the stream of evolution, the emergence of a SEEKING system motivates animals "to seek out energetically, to investigate and explore their worlds, to seek available resources and to make sense of the contingencies in their environments" (Panksepp 1998, 145). Eventually, Panksepp proposes, as they combine with increasingly elaborate cognitive and emotional mechanisms, SEEKING systems "give us the impulse to become actively engaged with the world and to extract meaning from our various circumstances" (Panksepp 1998, 145).

Although Barrett would take issue with this formulation of SEEKING or *interest* as a specific affect, it maps exactly onto her own definition of one of the dimensions of affect, what she calls *arousal*, or "how calm or agitated you feel"

(Barrett 2017, 72). "The energized feeling of anticipating good news, the jittery feeling after drinking too much coffee, the fatigue after a long run, and the weariness from lack of sleep are examples of high and low arousal," she suggests, are all *affect* (Barrett 2017, 72). Arousal corresponds to the continuum of caffeination, from a pleasant, barely perceptible shine on the edges of things to a jittery chaos of jagged lines. Barrett, too, correlates this to the brain's ongoing monitoring of a body's energy needs, an evolved mechanism that would seem to neatly map onto Panksepp's template.

From this perspective, the register of *becoming* is not *pure* becoming, but a highly refined set of neurophysiological mechanisms that register some of the jolts of novelty that crash against animal bodies – sometimes with excitement, sometimes with terror, annoyance, or frustration. Some bodies are more aggressive than others in harvesting the affects of novelty and change. Barrett points to research showing younger American adults are drawn to a compound of pleasant sensations and high arousal, whereas middle-aged and older Americans are drawn to pleasant sensations compounded with low arousal (Barrett 2017, 74). But even the most voracious consumer of arousal has limits: bombard a body with unpredictable noises and it will start out somewhat interested, but eventually take to drink – anything to escape the haze of glittering static. What the Deleuzian idiom of affect theory names *affect* as such, the register of becoming, is better understood as *one particular affect among many*: Deleuzian "affect" is *interest-excitement*, the structured, biologically grounded but historically tuned phenomenology of novelty.

Affect in the Tomkins and phenomenological dialects, then, attends to animality by enabling a consideration of the biological configurations that articulate bodies to formations of power. The complex, polymorphous biological template of experience is the plane of interface that makes relationality possible, not a pure principle of becoming. Elizabeth Wilson points out that "[f]eminism has thought of biology more as a site of stasis and predetermination, and less as a source of variation, differentiality, and conversion" and proposes that in order to understand, for instance, the political implications of new treatments for depression, we need to focus on the physiological localization of antidepressant medication in the gut (Wilson 2008, 374). I propose that affect theory enriches the analytics of power by massively expanding this template. How is our world shaped by our biologically potentialized appreciation of rhythm and rhyme, our sensitivity to color, the formulas of our neurochemistry, our susceptibility to other people's laughter, or our fascination with expressive faces? Different species will think and feel differently. How do formations of power engage differently with different animals? The model of affect as becoming has only limited ways of engaging this. The animality of affect is the animality of politics not in Massumi's sense of the politics of becoming, the event, or excess, but a material politics driven by the commingling of heterogeneous bodily forms.

4 Economies of Dignity: Reconsidering the Mosque Movement

Taken alone, phenomenology and psychology risk insufficient attention to both bodily specificity and to power. These are exactly the limitations the Tomkins and phenomenological dialects of affect theory set out to overcome. The body is not simply found, but – to a significant extent – made, an assemblage of co-constitutive learned and biological elements. What Tomkins and Sedgwick suggest is that embodied life plays out along the lines of flexible emotional architectures. Ahmed offers a theory of recursivity, a model of the way that the world rolls into the body, changes the body – which then reemerges changed into the world, reshaping the world itself. There's a productive junction here with work in the history of emotions, such as William Reddy's concept of *emotives* – statements about how one is feeling that have a simultaneous self-exploratory and self-altering capacity (Reddy 2004, 105). Like Reddy's work, affect theory is allied with performance theory in its concern with the dynamic of sedimentation and force. It is this mobile specificity, this liquid concreteness of the body that needs to be taken into account for the analytics of power. The phenomenological is political.

This approach is necessary to produce an account of the multiplicity of power relations rather than a binary of "affective" vs "non-affective" politics. Ahmed's work is particularly helpful in theorizing this. Rather than a narrow under-standing of affect, Ahmed suggests that we consider the way that the plurality of experienced emotions is configured in political formations, what she calls *affective economies*. In her 2004 essay of that title, Ahmed describes how the association of affects with objects – including other bodies – builds those objects into political frameworks (Ahmed 2004a, 128). For instance, the fear attached to some bodies, such as refugees, makes them a target of violent hostility. If we only talk about power as "affective" or "not-affective," the political texture of *this particular affect* becomes invisible. The allure and excitement of, for instance, a populist political movement appears in our field of vision, but we lose the ability to see how *different* formations of populism play out in *different* power-affect architectures.

There's no shortage of examples of how an understanding of affect as an embodied multiplicity illuminates the dynamics of power. José Esteban Muñoz has argued that a racialized regimen of power is often instantiated as the distribution of affective permissions: "Acting white has everything to do with the performance of a particular affect, the specific performance of which grounds the subject performing white affect in a normative life world," he writes. "Latinas and Latinos, and other people of color, are unable to achieve this affective performativity on a regular basis" (Muñoz 2000, 68). Deborah Gould's *Moving Politics* – an extraordinary hybrid of institutional autobiography and ethnography based on her experiences as an activist with ACT UP Chicago in the 1980s and 90s – pays lip service to a definition of affect as "unfixed, unstructured, noncoherent, and nonlinguistic" (Gould 2009, 20) – alongside a statement of commitment to the Tomkins dialect. But her actual analysis largely discards the Deleuzian vocabulary, focusing on emotions – shame, pride, and despair. Tracking affect exclusively in terms of becoming misses this specificity of texture. And it doesn't make sense to talk about the political effects of depression in Ann Cvetkovich's work, for instance, outside the dialect that identifies it as a specific, bodily grounded affect. What Cvetkovich describes as the depressive phenomenology of the impasse – both its creation against the backdrop of late capitalism and its corrosive effects on individual bodies and political movements – must be diagrammed in its emotional particularity (Cvetkovich 2012, 20–1).

For the remainder of this section, I want to focus on how this approach can be used as a touchstone to revisit one of the most salient studies in contemporary theory, Saba Mahmood's *The Politics of Piety*. I propose that Mahmood's dialogues with the participants in the Egyptian mosque movement offer more than a critique of a liberal discourse of naturally free subjects; it also poses the necessity of setting political-religious movements against the backdrop of overarching affective economies.

Economies of Dignity

Some poststructuralist and feminist philosophers of religion have made becoming a central analytic category in the exploration of religion. Grace Jantzen, for instance, emphasizes the "strategic value in rethinking religion rather than in acquiescing in an already masculinized secularism, not 'awaiting the god passively, but bringing the god to life through us'" (Jantzen 1999, 275). This recasting of religion as *becoming-divine* is what she calls "the *process* of divinity" (Jantzen 1999, 255). My argument is that seeing religion as fundamentally about becoming is insufficient for understanding religion in its animality. Pure religion, the religion of becoming, the religion of affect rather than affects, risks leaving the body behind, or at least limiting religion to a narrow band of encounters with novelty.

To illustrate the specific relevance of these dialects of affect theory for religion, I want to conjoin Ahmed's notion of the affective economy to

Sedgwick's consideration of the analytics of shame. Rather than aligning directly with Sedgwick's model of queer performativity – in which *shame* is illuminated as a productive resource – the dialogue with Mahmood's work will explore how a dynamic of *aversive* shame and a thirst to restore dignity structures political and religious formations. My contention is that what we can call an *economy of dignity* is a situation in which bodies make decisions on the basis of the felt need to assert dignity or to repudiate shame – rather than through the liberal tropes of free choice, economic benefit, or political power.

For Tomkins, shame is a labile but profoundly powerful affective configuration. "Though terror speaks to life and death," he writes, "and distress makes of the world a vale of tears, yet shame strikes deepest into the heart of man" (Tomkins 1995, 133). We see in this formula Tomkins's indication of how shame dynamics overrun the cost-benefit calculations of the liberal subject. What Tomkins calls a *shame theory* – a strategy for negating shame – can be so powerful that it overwhelms even core directives like survival. "One can frighten the soldier out of cowardice," Tomkins muses, "by making him more afraid of cowardice than death" (Tomkins 1995, 57). Or, to take the same postulate from the other side, dignity can be such an electrifying affect that it overthrows fear of death. The compulsory force of an economy of dignity can drive bodies to move at oblique angles to flourishing, fitness, or financial benefit.

We see an illustration of this animal approach to politics in Reddy's work on the runway to the Revolution in early modern France. Reddy proposes that the antecedent to the Revolutionary moment can be understood not just as a ferment of political institutions or class struggle, but as a tectonic cascade of emotional forces embedded in a dynamic affective economy. The catalyst for this is the new aristocratic culture built by Louis XIV. Nobles in Louis's orbit were subjected to a thick regime of what Reddy calls *emotional management*. He writes that "a newly elaborated set of norms of emotional expression" operating under the heading of "civility" created, in effect, a form of policing that supplemented the bureaucratic regime of the king (Reddy 2004, 147). Louis XIV's confinement of the aristocracy at Versailles and his imposition of an elaborate ceremonial and etiquette regimen allowed him to much more effectively control them.

But, as Foucault's analytics of power predicts, this emotional regimentation was not simply a top-down, negative imposition: it worked by enticing the aristocracy's emotional investment in the system. The aristocracy fell in line, Reddy suggests, not only because he increased their material prosperity, but because he centralized them in an economy of dignity that elevated them above others: the aristocrats "won" by becoming a hub for "the subtle but unmistakable marks of deference in the manners of those around them," Reddy writes. "The new etiquette organized the whole country into a single series of cascades of disdain" (Reddy 2004, 148). In Ahmed's terms, the order of civility was an affective economy, and in particular an economy of dignity. Through radial networks of deference, aristocrats found themselves accumulating dignity in the form of emotive tributes offered by their inferiors. Louis XIV cemented power by organizing his court into a pyramidal economy of dignity.

Saba Mahmood's description in *The Politics of Piety* of the women's mosque movement in prerevolutionary Egypt offers a case study of how such an economy of dignity works in detail. Mahmood did her fieldwork in Cairo in the mid-1990s with groups of women who were fomenting an Islamic revival from their mosques across the city. These women discussed Islamic texts and teachings and consumed Islamic media. A particular focus of this expanding network of conversations was the creation of dispositions or habits, embodied practices that were thought to cultivate particular virtues. Building on the last interview of Michel Foucault, "On the Genealogy of Ethics," Mahmood examined the way that these embodied practices constituted a set of self-imposed technologies of the self, or *ethics*. These technologies – such as the wearing of the hijab – were designed to reshape the landscape of embodied dispositions of ethical agents, transforming them, in this instance, into better Islamic subjects.

As Mahmood writes, however, this project from the outset played out as "a set of puzzles" inherited from her work in feminist and progressive politics (Mahmood 2005, ix). The central puzzle, from the perspective of her training Western liberal feminist, is that the wearing of the hijab and other practices of conservative Islam appeared to be patriarchal impositions forced on women in order to constrain their sexuality. Liberal feminism, Mahmood observes, views the self-directed practice of veiling as a projection of the false consciousness of women so alienated from their own innate thirst for liberation that they have internalized the oppressive coordinates of patriarchy. The liberal feminist position could only affirm that women who revived conservative forms of Islam were mindlessly amplifying their own oppression.

The problem, from Mahmood's perspective, is that this approach ended up replicating a colonial political project. It presented a set of western values as universal and dismissed as deluded or deceived any perspective that did not conform to that project. The ontology of a naturally freedom-seeking agent, Mahmood shows, is a metaphysical presupposition of the Enlightenment (Mahmood 2005, 14). Moreover, the confidence of the Enlightenment posture that it is the only highway to a just society is betrayed by the brutal history of

European colonization even after the Enlightenment – even and especially as the Enlightenment was invoked to justify European global sovereignty and numb the response to atrocities committed in its name. From Mahmood's perspective, the critiques of the hijab and Islamism generally by Western feminists unwittingly replicated this oppressive logic, lapsing into the self-serving attempt to save brown women from brown men (Mahmood 2005, 199).

Mahmood's argument is that in order to assess the actions of the women in the mosque movement in a way that empowers participants, feminism must open itself up to a view of agency that supersedes the limited repertoire of Enlightenment liberalism. Foucault's analytics of power, she writes, "encourages us to conceptualize agency not simply as a synonym for resistance to relations of domination, but as a capacity for action that specific relations of *subordination* create and enable" (Mahmood 2005, 18). Agency is not a transcendental property, but a dimension of bodily activity embedded within a particular set of material circumstances. By these lights, "what may appear to be a case of deplorable passivity and docility from a progressivist point of view, may actually be a form of agency" (Mahmood 2005, 15). The presumed convergence between agency and liberal secular values that structures Western feminist critiques of Islam overlooks the way that Muslim women devise their own formations of agency within the circumstances of their situation.

The question, however, is whether stepping away from the binary of resistance/domination is sufficient to disrupt liberalism. The risk is that even a pluralized *agency* is still pinned to a preeminently liberal category. I want to suggest another interpretative framing of Mahmood's ethnography. Rather than focusing on individual agency as a good in itself, I argue that religious bodies are making decisions with reference to an overarching affective economy. In this case, the Piety Movement can best be understood as the unfolding of an economy of dignity, guiding bodies to a set of embodied practices that elicit dignity as a distinct affective structure.

Mahmood writes that "the mosque movement had emerged in response to the perception that religious knowledge, as a means of organizing daily conduct, had become increasingly marginalized under modern structures of secular governance" (Mahmood 2005, 4). It tapped into the same affective ferment that would eventually erupt in the Tahrir Square uprising of 2011: a sense that the corrupt, US-backed military government of Hosni Mubarak was not only plundering the country, but holding their citizenry in contempt while they did so. The *New York Times* journalist Anthony Shadid quoted a young hijabi activist during the Tahrir Square uprising: "This is our country," she declared. "We want to stay in our country. We want to share in its wealth, we want to be part of its land. They can only laugh at us so long, make fun of us for so long" (Shadid 2011). The Tahrir uprising was primarily political rather than religious, like the Mosque Movement, but it would seem the feeling of ongoing degradation by a callous elite provided motivational force in both cases.

This is why so much of the work done by Mahmood's consultants is emotional. Fear is often part of this affective self-labor. "The rhetorical style employed by the three dā'iyāt [preachers]," Mahmood observes, "relies heavily on the technique of invoking fear (*tarhīb*), an emotion invoked through colorful and graphic depictions of God's wrath, the contortions of death, and the tortures of hell. Women often react with loud exclamations, followed by loud incantations of the gory details of the torture and religious chants to ward off the anticipated pain and evil" (Mahmood 2005, 91). Mahmood describes one of her consultants, Hajja Samira, as producing affectively rich narratives that constitute the religious subject as an epic figure avoiding the fires of hell through the diligent cultivation of her own pious self (Mahmood 2005, 144). Charles Hirschkind, carrying out parallel fieldwork in Egypt in the same time period, describes an interviewee admiring a cassette sermon and observing, "That preacher must be Saudi. They're the ones who really know how to scare you" (Hirschkind 2006, 1). Fear is a necessary ingredient of this affective economy. It provides a channel of pressure that, when artfully combined with a horizon of hopeful release, helps to propel participants along the trajectory of self-cultivation.

Similarly, Mahmood's consultants describe the vital necessity of cultivating the virtue of shyness, or modesty. This is explored as a process of behaving shyly in order to change one's internal emotional disposition. A woman interviewed by Mahmood says, "[I] realized that al-ḥayā' was among the good deeds ..., and given my natural lack of shyness ... I had to make or create it first. I realized that making ... it in yourself is not hypocrisy, and that eventually your inside learns to have al-ḥayā' too'" (Mahmood 2005, 156). In other words, the physical performance of an emotional disposition eventually came to inculcate the disposition itself. Mahmood observes that "it is through repeated *bodily acts* that one trains one's memory, desire, and intellect to behave according to established standards of conduct" (Mahmood 2005, 157). As Monique Scheer has artfully argued, emotions can be understood as a kind of practice, or *habitus* in Pierre Bourdieu's term: emotions change "not only because norms, expectations, words, and concepts that shape experience are modified, but also because the practices in which they are embodied, and bodies themselves, undergo transformation" (Scheer 2012, 220). The bodily practices developed within the mosque movement exert exactly this shaping role on participants' emotional states.[14]

This brings us to a vital point: the affective self-work of the mosque movement women is not about evanescent becoming, excess, or a disruptive *event*. Rather, it's about sustained, disciplined labor that produces durable bodily transformations. Mahmood's contention is that we need to move beyond a position – represented in both liberal and poststructuralist perspectives – that the only valid thing women can do with conservative power formations is resist them. "Norms are not only consolidated and/or subverted," she writes, "but performed, inhabited, and experienced in a variety of ways" (Mahmood 2005, 22). Similarly, a model of affect as becoming offers very little, if anything, to thinking about the magnetic attraction of conservative movements. The revivification of conservatism may, in some sense, be a novelty – and this novelty may even be part of its affective field, in line with the phenomenology of novelty – but this is not what makes it work. The romantic framing of affect as the slipstream of becoming misses the vital lure of nostalgia, the fascination with images, techniques, and facets of history that are not new, but capture the stony gravity of history.

This concern with power as a modality of sustained affective transformation is already present in the late Foucault, especially "On the Genealogy of Ethics," which finds Foucault snickering at liberation movements which have become so liberated that they have abandoned the techniques of the self, or *ethics*, that provided previous political movements with a center of gravity: "They need an ethics, but they cannot find any other ethics than an ethics founded on so-called scientific knowledge of what the self is, what desire is, what the unconscious is, and so on" (Foucault 1984, 343). He calls for a reconsideration of classical technologies of the self, including not only careful self-scrutiny, but disciplinary practices like sexual austerity, which he describes as "a philosophical movement coming from very cultivated people in order to give to their life much more intensity, much more beauty" (Foucault 1984, 349). Building on the assertion that power, of necessity, both produces and constrains, Foucault contends that self-fashioning – often through the channel of self-denial – is an instrument for the production of power and beauty.

This is precisely what Mahmood finds among the mosque movement followers. They saw the failure of Islam in Egyptian society as, in part, a result of a misconception of the religion as a sort of folk culture rather than as a mechanism for the training and transfiguration of the self (Mahmood 2005,

---

[14] These are "emotives," in a sense, but it's worth noting that Reddy seems to exclusively understand emotives as statements, thereby overlooking the way that embodied gestures can also have "a self-exploring or self-altering effect" (Reddy 2004, 100).

48). "Among mosque participants," Mahmood found, "individual efforts toward self-realization are aimed not so much at discovering one's 'true' desires and feelings, or at establishing a personal relationship with God, but at honing one's rational and emotional capacities so as to approximate the exemplary model of the pious self" (Mahmood 2005, 31). Rather than Kantian moral subjects choosing from the zero-point of pure rationality, Mahmood retraces the entanglement of Islamic and Aristotelian intellectual traditions emphasizing the cultivation of durable virtues and, ultimately, rigorous attachments, what she terms, in her later essay "Religious Reason and Secular Affect," *schesis* (Mahmood 2005, 27; see also Mahmood 2009, 847). This sense of affective transformation, too, is not about becoming, but sedimentation – the accumulation of durable affective structures that reshape the contours of the self. The vocabulary of becoming can't shed any light on these processes of self-empowerment.

The retrieval of a set of religious lifeways that distinguished politically disenfranchised women from a stiflingly aloof ruling class and reconstituted them as religious bodies set apart from the world offered a strategy for affirming dignity in the face of everyday degradation. It articulated their bodies to a set of cultural formations suffused with confidence, majesty, and glory. It seems likely that this interlocked with a felt resistance to the global Euro-American hegemony propping up the Egyptian dictator. Tomkins writes that "we may expect the emergence of counter-terror and counter-humiliation and counter-distress – to repay the former colonial powers for past shame, terror, and suffering" (Tomkins 1995, 73). The return to Islamism is, in part, an expression of defiance, an embodied gesture in a global affective economy that develops the dignity of the religious bodies involved.

Religion often serves this function of a perpetual dignity machine. The doctrinal and moral content of religion operates as a set of struts for building up an embodied sense of dignity.

I see this analysis as, in a sense, an expansion of the register of detail of Mahmood's approach. Where Mahmood affirms that we need an analytics that allows for multiple forms of agency, my suggestion is that "agency" and the seizing of agency is very often an affective maneuver within an economy of dignity. It is not the individual body that has agency, but the affects moving through the body. These affects need to be understood in the plural, rather than according to the singular logic of becoming. Tracking *becoming* can tell us that change is happening. It can't tell us how power is actually shaping the interface between bodies and their historical circumstances.

Hirschkind interprets the affective registers of the cassette sermons in circulation among Egypt's Islamist subcultures as affective scaffolding imported to flesh out a picture of what an Islamic society should look like. "As opposed to television," Hirschkind writes, "through which one falls into the 'animality of instincts,' tapes provide a sonorous environment where the nourishing, trans-formative power of ethical speech works to improve the conditions of one's heart, fortifying the moral sensibilities that, in accord with Islamic ethical traditions, incline toward right actions" (Hirschkind 2006, 10). I would invert this and suggest that what we're really seeing is a conceptual agenda *driven by affects*. There is no non-affective ethical speech, only different formations of affect mediated through different technological forms. We *become* religious (or secular) through the pulses of an affective economy; we do not coolly select affects in order to become religious.

As Tomkins writes, "shame is an affect of relatively high toxicity . . . it strikes deepest into the heart of man . . . it is felt as a sickness of the soul which leaves man naked, defeated, alienated, and lacking in dignity" (Tomkins 1995, 148). Dignity is not cosmetic; it is psychological oxygen. Bodies will fight to build affective economies that nurture and sustain dignity and expel shame. Religion seems to be especially well-suited to play this part. But an approach to affect that locks it into the realm of becoming misses these patterns. It focuses exclusively on lines of flight, on flare-ups of novelty. This produces a theory of power that is oblivious to the power of discipline to cultivate durable bodily dispositions, to the vivid textures of affective economies, and to the scintillating appeal of conservative political and spiritual formations.

Conclusion: The Entertainment

David Foster Wallace's near-future sci-fi novel *Infinite Jest* is about desire, especially the way our sense of sovereignty over self is eclipsed by the rigid skein of desires that really pull our strings. Often, these forms of desire are tragic addictions – hard drugs and alcohol – but there are many others: "yoga, reading, politics, gum-chewing, crossword puzzles, solitaire, romantic intrigue, charity work, political activism, N.R.A. membership, music, art, cleaning, plastic surgery, cartridge-viewing even at normal distances, the loyalty of a fine dog, religious zeal, relentless helpfulness, relentless other-folks'-moral-inventory-taking, the development of hard-line schools of 12-Step thought, ad darn near infinitum, including 12-Step fellowships themselves . . . " (Wallace 1996, 998, en. 70).

The title of the novel is taken from the name of a video cartridge that circulates in the background of the plot, driving geopolitical events that are largely irrelevant to the everyday lives of the main characters. The cartridge, sometimes referred to simply as "The Entertainment," shows a film that produces a fanatical, unyielding desire in all who watch it. The desire is to watch more of The Entertainment. It's so powerful that it's literally fatal, outshining bodily needs such as eating and drinking, leaving chains of catatonic bodies gazing drooling at screens wherever it's shown. An FBI agent laments the loss of a colleague who was exposed: "Twenty-year man, Hank. Damn good man. He was a friend. He's in four-point restraints now. Nourishment through a tube. No desire or even basic survival-type will for anything other than more view-ing" (Wallace 1996, 507).

Over the course of the novel, we come to learn that The Entertainment is, in fact, a carefully choreographed avant-garde film directed by James Incandenza, the mysterious late father of protagonist Hal Incandenza. It's the ultimate addiction. Like a permanent electrical surge, it breaks the affective economies of bodies, leveling them down to a single point of relentless, obsessive focus: "The persons' lives' meanings had collapsed to such a narrow focus that no other activity or connection could hold their attention. Possessed of roughly the mental/spiritual energies of a moth, now, according to a diagnostician out of C. D.C" (Wallace 1996, 549). A moth clumsily slamming its body against a brilliantly incandescent light.

Infinite Jest works as a sort of thought experiment for affect theory. What is this thing that is so wanted? What chain of images move bodies so deeply that they become radically fixated on it and will pursue it at all costs? Wallace's own answer is a snarky philosophical joke: we learn over the course of the novel that "The Mad Stork" Incandenza had unlocked a secret visual formula that tapped into the deepest stratum of human need. The Entertainment starts with a veiled woman recognizing a person in a revolving door in a lobby. It then cuts to an infant's-eye-view, looking up from a crib at the unveiled woman, possibly with her face digitally modulated. Speaking into the camera, she says Death is always female, and the female who kills you in your previous life becomes your mother in the next life. She then apologizes, over and over and over again. The infant's view is shot with a special lens designed to replicate the optical perspective of a newborn. The film, then, takes the ur-memory – looking up at one's mother – and reconfigures it into the ultimate psychic need – her apology for having taken your life before your birth. It's a viciously deft parody of psychoanalysis – or maybe not. In the final analysis, like so much else in the novel, the meaning is coyly undecidable.

I'm not so much interested in Wallace's answer as I am interested in simulat-ing The Entertainment as a philosophical experiment to shed light on the different dialects of affect theory. If we understand affect as becoming, what is The Entertainment? It would be a permanent field of change, a vortex of unceasing visual noise. It would amount to a colorized version of television static – the hissing snow of an analog set detuned from all channels. Signal static is, in actuality, the convergence of countless sources of atmospheric electrical noise picked up by the TV set: distant storms, cosmic background radiation, and the atmospheric effects of solar flares crash together around us all the time. They are rendered visible/audible by an antenna designed to convert signals into images and sounds. It is, in short, Weather Patterns on a vast scale, with a farther-reaching antenna tuned to electrical signals rather than the physical signals caused by bodies and air currents moving through the space. As Massumi writes, "[i]ntensity is qualifiable as an emotional state, and that state is static – temporal and narrative noise . . . . It is not exactly passivity, because it is filled with motion, vibratory motion, resonation" (Massumi 2002, 26). From the perspective of affect as becoming, static would be the ultimate form of desire, an irresistibly erotic field of flux.

But we know this isn't right. Bodies don't want noise. They want movement, yes, and novelty, but movement within a structured field. We want ballet, symphony, chiaroscuro, cinema – not prismatic TV static. A play of forms keyed to the pulse and rhythm of our bodies, our memories, our worlds. Not pure play. This is why the student lingering on the fringes of *Weather Patterns* takes to drink. The interest value of raw noise for a body is sharply limited. What Weather Patterns models is an *ontology* – a vision of the dynamic interactions of *substance*. It does this exceptionally well. What it does not model is power – that which makes bodies move.

But for the Tomkins and phenomenological dialects of affect theory, bodies can't be solved for like an equation. There are too many contingencies, too many layers of the plastic and the rigid, too many dice rolls. It would be like solving chess. There is no The Entertainment. This is how Sedgwick falls in love with the litany of *if-may* statements as a genre: they map the balletic contingencies of embodied life. To understand power – the dendritic watercourses of where our bodies go, carved out of fields of force – we need to start from this recognition that our animal existence is a multifaceted fusion of the biological and the historical. Elizabeth A. Wilson calls this *gut feminism*, "a feminist theory that is able to think innovatively and organically at the same time" (Wilson 2015, 17). It's a platform for reconciliation between the science and the humanities, but keyed to the question of power, a concern proper to the humanities.

If there must be a distinction between affect and emotion, my sense is that Sianne Ngai's version offers the most promise. In Ngai's work, the difference between affect and emotion is taken as a modal difference of intensity or degree, rather than a formal difference of quality or kind. My assumption is that affects are *less* formed and structured than emotions, but not lacking form or structure altogether; *less* "sociolinguistically fixed," but by no means code-free or meaningless; *less* "organized in response to our interpretations of situations," but by no means entirely devoid of organization or diagnostic powers. (Ngai 2005, 27)

Ngai, like Lisa Feldman Barrett, suggests that affect-emotion is best understood as a continuum from micro to macro, rather than a different register altogether (Barrett 2017, 72). Moreover, for Ngai (less so for Barrett), these affective particles merge into emotional architectures with distinct forms and patterns – and therefore distinct ways of fitting bodies into force fields of power. Affect is not on/off; it's always present, always humming through the immanent field of power relations. The first rule of this stance is: nothing is without affective charge. The second is: nothing we consume offers a single "affect." A film, for instance, is a narrative package, an ensemble of rich colors, beautiful faces and bodies, clever words, familiar symbols, novel images and configurations. The task of tracking power is the task of diagramming this plurality of affective forms and how they fascinate bodies.

I think there's an equally strong case to be made for a tactical imprecision in the way we use these words – a deliberate blurring of affect/emotion/feeling, as Ann Cvetkovich suggests. These terms can point to a zone of indistinction rather than precise, technical division. This has the advantage of reflecting the current unsettled state of the psychology of emotions. The field of emotion science is a fascinating resource for reflection in the humanities. But emotion science is also in a state of acute flux. Engagements with the sciences from the humanities do well to carefully frame those areas where a live debate is going on, and should be extremely cautious about resolutely adjudicating data-driven disputes. To overstate the conclusions of the psychology of emotions today would be to fall down on this responsibility. This is why affect theory can talk about emotions without fully committing to the Basic Emotions hypothesis as such. But mostly, the humanities benefits by drafting ideas and theories from the sciences into conversations in the humanities – such as the study of power.

Humanists can engage – vigorously – with the life sciences as a set of materials for developing theoretical perspectives within their own research. These encounters should be couched in caveats about the distance humanities scholars necessarily have from laboratory contexts, and even from the mainstream of peer-reviewed journal publication. As Jan Plamper points out, the dynamic between the sciences and the humanities is troubled, in part, because of the varying speed of publication in those two fields – very fast peer-reviewed experimental research versus slow-moving interpretative books that often rely on popularizations of scientific conversations (Plamper 2015, 241–2). Plamper further suggests that humanities scholars should familiarize themselves not only with the basics of experiment design, but with the different genres of science writing – original research articles, review articles, popularizations – and the offerings and limitations of each (Plamper 2015, 298). Lastly, humanities scholars should acknowledge the extent to which a scientific theory under study is contentious. "Settled science" doesn't mean that there aren't dissenters, only that a mainstream consensus seems to have emerged.

The contribution of the humanities to the sciences is, in turn, often a matter of identifying areas where the sciences have unwittingly imported the debris of past debates in the humanities that have found their way into common sense – the category of *consciousness* is one example, a concept developed in the early modern period to try to provide metaphysical underpinnings for rapidly changing epistemological frames. The question isn't whether affects are above or below the water line of consciousness. The question is how that line is made – and how it is constantly being redrawn. To be "conscious" is always a moving target. What are "you" aware of? Are you aware, moment to moment, that you're tired, that you're seething, that you're elated? What happens when you reflect on your own sensations – do they change? What happens when someone asks you how you're doing – do you change? What happens when you answer with an emotive statement that, as Reddy points out, simultaneously communicates and alters your emotional makeup?

The self as a pulsing mass of affects produces subjectivity. The cloud of *awareness* that floats through this mass and gets called "consciousness" is downstream of this pulse. Against the metaphysics of consciousness practiced by both Massumi (the rigid bounding line of the personal) and Leys (the horizon of the intact self), I propose the wholesale replacement of the term *consciousness* with something like *processes of mentation and sensation*. Sometimes a process of mentation/sensation detects another process of mentation/sensation. What gets called "consciousness" is a braiding together of these filaments of mind. Consciousness, then, isn't an on/off switch but a field of twisting forces that sometimes twist back on themselves, creating an illusion of global self-awareness that is, in fact, material and contingent.

Some scholars propose that affect is best understood as resistant to any sort of systematization or methodological improvement. I consider this to be worryingly aristocratic, locking affect theory into a permanent mistiness. There's no trajectory of refinement, as we would hope to see in any other academic conversation – only a delight in the play of wispy ideas. There's an argument waiting in the wings that the refusal of systematization is a way of repudiating the neoliberalization of the university. But it's not enough to be anything-but-capitalist. Aristocratic elitism that fundamentally refuses the value of labor – in the way that nineteenth-century bourgeoisie who wanted to establish themselves as quasi-gentry insisted on being photographed without tools or implements of trade – is also non-capitalist. That would seem to be the risk of self-consciously unuseful or opaque academic work. Another form of resistance dignifies labor – including intellectual labor – as the task of making things that work. In the case of academic labor in the humanities, that means making ideas that help to better diagnose, understand, and intervene in formations of power. Theory can't be a conceptual abstract sculpture garden. It's incumbent on affect theorists to try to understand the present moment. The Bergsonian strand of Deleuze's thought, I have argued, does not have sufficient resources for this enterprise.

How can a face shape political life? Why do we like music that is without words? This is what it means to be a body – to be an animal – and to be susceptible to power. Affect theory proposes that affects are the living matter of subjectivity. The surfacing of affects enables a new level of precision in Foucault's project of the analytics of power. In order to fully capture this precision, affects must be defined in their specificity – as templates emerging out of biological histories that articulate bodies to formations of power in specific ways. In this sense, affects are best understood as animal. They are organic inheritances from our animal genealogies, just as other animal bodies have their own semi-stable affective architectures. At the same time, they are the sovereign engines of our experience and our decision-making, inherently multiple, but each advancing a set of intransigent priorities. Affective economies emerge in the tension between these multiple affective priorities, and religion, like other formations of power, is an effect of these dynamics.

Bibliography

Ahmed, Sara. "Affective Economies." *Social Text 79* 22.2 (Summer 2004a): 117–39.

Ahmed, Sara. "Collective Feelings, Or, The Impressions Left by Others." *Theory, Culture & Society* 21.2 (2004b): 25–42.

Ahmed, Sara. *The Cultural Politics of Emotion*. New York, NY: Routledge, 2004c.

Ahmed, Sara. *Queer Phenomenology: Orientations, Objects, Others*. Durham, NC: Duke University Press, 2006.

Ahmed, Sara. *The Promise of Happiness*. Durham, NC: Duke University Press, 2010.

Badiou, Alain. *Ethics*. Hallward, Peter, trans. London: Verso, 2001.

Badiou, Alain. *Saint Paul: The Foundation of Universalism*. Stanford, CA: Stanford University Press, 2003.

Barrett, Lisa Feldman. How Emotions Are Made: The Secret Life of the Brain. New York, NY: Houghton Mifflin Harcourt, 2017.

Beatty, John. "Reconsidering the Importance of Chance Variation." In Massimo Pigliucci and Gerd B. Müller, eds. *Evolution: The Extended Synthesis*. Cambridge, MA: Massachusetts Institute of Technology Press, 2010: 21–44.

Bennett, Jane. *Vibrant Matter: A Political Ecology of Things*. Durham, NC: Duke University Press, 2010.

Breland, Keller and Marian Breland. "The Misbehavior of Organisms." *American Psychologist* 16 (1961): 681–4.

Brinkema, Eugenie. *The Forms of the Affects*. Durham, NC: Duke University Press, 2014.

Browne, Janet. *Charles Darwin: The Power of Place*. New York, NY: Knopf, 2002.

Center for 21st Century Studies. "The Nonhuman Turn." 2012. Available at: www4.uwm.edu/c21/pdfs/conferences/2012_nonhumanturn/NHT_Program .pdf Accessed October 13, 2018.

Chen, Mel Y. *Animacies: Biopolitics, Racial Mattering, and Queer Affect*. Durham, NC: Duke University Press, 2012.

Cixous, Hélène and Mireille Calle-Gruber. *Rootprints: Memory and Life Writing*. Prenowitz, Eric, trans. London: Routledge, 1997.

Connolly, William E. "The Complexity of Intention." *Critical Inquiry* 37.4 (Summer 2011): 791–8.

Cvetkovich, Ann. *Depression: A Public Feeling*. Durham, NC: Duke University Press, 2012.

Damasio, Antonio R. *Descartes' Error: Emotion, Reason, and the Human Brain*. New York, NY: Putnam, 1994.

Damasio, Antonio. *The Feeling of What Happens: Body and Emotion in the Making of Consciousness*. New York, NY: Harcourt, 1999.

Darwin, Charles. *The Descent of Man and Selection in Relation to Sex*. 2nd ed. London: John Murray, 1882.

Darwin, Charles. *The Expression of the Emotions in Man and Animals*. Joe Cain and Sharon Messenger, eds. London: Penguin Books, 2009.

Darwin, Charles. *The Origin of Species by Means of Natural Selection, or the Preservation of Favoured Races in the Struggle for Life*. 6th edition, with additions and corrections. London: John Murray, 1876.

de Waal, Frans. *Our Inner Ape: A Leading Primatologist Explains Why We Are Who We Are*. New York, NY: Riverhead Books, 2005.

Deleuze, Gilles. *Bergsonism*. Tomlinson, Hugh, and Barbara Habberjam, trans. New York, NY: Zone Books, 1988a.

Deleuze, Gilles. *Spinoza: Practical Philosophy*. Hurley, Robert, trans. San Francisco, CA: City Lights Books, 1988b.

Deleuze, Gilles. *Expressionism in Philosophy: Spinoza*. Joughin, Martin, trans. New York, NY: Zone Books, 1990.

Deleuze, Gilles and Felix Guattari. *A Thousand Plateaus: Capitalism and Schizophrenia*. Massumi, Brian, trans. Minneapolis, MN: University of Minnesota Press, 1987.

Deleuze, Gilles and Felix Guattari. *What is Philosophy?* Tomlinson, Hugh, and Graham Burchell, trans. New York, NY: Columbia University Press, 1994.

Derrida, Jacques. *The Animal That Therefore I Am*. Wills, David, trans. New York, NY: Fordham University Press, 2008.

Descartes, René. "The Passions of the Soul." In Gerald W. Marshall, ed. *The Restoration Mind*. Cranbury, NJ: Associated University Presses, 1997: 325–404.

Foucault, Michel. "On the Genealogy of Ethics: An Overview of Work in Progress." In Rabinow, Paul Rabinow, ed. *The Foucault Reader*. New York, NY: Pantheon Books, 1984: 340–72.

Foucault, Michel. *The History of Sexuality: Volume* One. Hurley, Robert, trans. New York, NY: Vintage Books, 1990.

Foucault, Michel. "The Subject and Power." In Hubert L. Dreyfus and Paul Rabinow, eds. *Michel Foucault: Beyond Structuralism and Hermeneutics*. 2nd edn. Chicago, IL: University of Chicago Press, 1982: 208–26.

Frank, Adam and Elizabeth A. Wilson. "Like-Minded." *Critical Inquiry* 38.4 (Summer 2012): 870–7.

Frost, Samantha. *Biocultural Creatures: Toward a New Theory of the Human.* Durham, NC: Duke University Press, 2016.

Gould, Deborah. *Moving Politics: Emotion and ACT UP's Fight against AIDS.* Chicago, IL: University of Chicago Press, 2009.

Gould, Stephen Jay. *The Structure of Evolutionary Theory.* Cambridge, MA: Belknap Press, 2002.

Gregg, Melissa and Gregory J. Seigworth. "An Inventory of Shimmers." In Melissa Gregg and Gregory J. Seigworth, eds. *The Affect Theory Reader.* Durham, NC: Duke University Press, 2010: 1–28.

Grosz, Elizabeth. *Volatile Bodies: Toward a Corporeal Feminism.* Bloomington and Indianapolis, IN: Indiana University Press, 1994.

Haraway, Donna J. *When Species Meet.* Minneapolis, MN: University of Minnesota Press, 2008.

Hardt, Michael. *Gilles Deleuze: An Apprenticeship in Philosophy.* Minneapolis, MN: University of Minnesota Press, 1993.

Hirschkind, Charles. *The Ethical Soundscape: Cassette Sermons and Islamic Counterpublics.* New York, NY: Columbia University Press, 2006.

Hrdy, Sarah Blaffer. *Mother Nature: A History of Mothers, Infants, and Natural Selection.* New York, NY: Pantheon Books, 1999.

Husserl, Edmund. *Ideas Pertaining to a Pure Phenomenology and to a Phenomenological Philosophy, Book 2.* Rojcewicz, Richard, and André Schuwer, trans. Dordrecht, the Netherlands: Kluwer Academic Publishers, 1987.

Jantzen, Grace M. *Becoming Divine: Towards a Feminist Philosophy of Religion.* Bloomington, IN: Indiana University Press, 1999.

Leys, Ruth. *The Ascent of Affect: Genealogy and Critique.* Chicago, IL: University of Chicago Press, 2017.

Leys, Ruth. "A Reply to William E. Connolly." *Critical Inquiry* 37.4 (Summer 2011): 799–805.

Leys, Ruth. "The Turn to Affect: A Critique." *Critical Inquiry* 37.3 (Spring 2011): 434–72.

Mahmood, Saba. *Politics of Piety: The Islamic Revival and the Feminist Subject.* Princeton, NJ and Oxford, UK: Princeton University Press, 2005.

Mahmood, Saba. "Religious Reason and Secular Affect: An Incommensurable Divide?" *Critical Inquiry* 35 (Summer 2009): 836–62.

Malabou, Catherine and Jacques Derrida. *Counterpath.* Wills, David, trans. Stanford, CA: Stanford University Press, 2004.

Manning, Erin. *Always More than One: Individuation's Dance*. Durham, NC: Duke University Press, 2013.

Manning, Erin. *Relationscapes: Movement, Art, Philosophy*. Cambridge, MA: MIT Press, 2009.

Margulis, Lynn. *The Symbiotic Planet: A New Look at Evolution*. London: Phoenix, 1998.

Massumi, Brian. *What Animals Teach Us about Politics*. Durham, NC: Duke University Press, 2014.

Massumi, Brian. *Parables for the Virtual: Movement, Affect, Sensation*. Durham, NC: Duke University Press, 2002.

Massumi, Brian. *A User's Guide to Capitalism and Schizophrenia: Deviations from Deleuze and Guattari*. Cambridge, MA: MIT Press, 1992.

Mazzarella, William. "Affect: What Is It Good For?" In Saurabh Dube, ed. *Enchantments of Modernity: Empire, Nation, Globalization*. London, New York, and New Delhi: Routledge, 2009: 291–309.

Merleau-Ponty, Maurice. *Phenomenology of Perception*. Smith, Colin, trans. New York, NY: Routledge, 1962.

Muñoz, José Esteban. "Feeling Brown: Ethnicity and Affect in Ricardo Bracho's 'The Sweetest Hangover (And Other STDs).'" *Theatre Journal* 52.1 (March 2000): 67–79.

Nathanson, Donald L. "Prologue: Affect Imagery Consciousness." In Tomkins, Silvan S. *Affect Imagery Consciousness: The Complete Edition*. Karon, Bertram P., ed. New York: Springer Publishing Company, 2008: xi–xxvi.

Ngai, Sianne. *Ugly Feelings*. Cambridge, MA: Harvard University Press, 2005.

Panksepp, Jaak. *Affective Neuroscience: The Foundations of Human and Animal Emotions*. Oxford, UK: Oxford University Press, 1998.

Papacharissi, Zizi. *Affective Publics: Sentiment, Technology, and Politics*. Oxford, UK: Oxford University Press, 2015.

Papoulias, Constantina, and Felicity Callard. "Biology's Gift: Interrogating the Turn to Affect." *Body & Society* 16.1 (2010): 29–56.

Pedwell, Carolyn. "Affect Theory's Alternative Genealogies: A Response to Ruth Leys." History of the Human Sciences (2019).

Pellegrini, Ann and Jasbir Puar. "Affect." *Social Text 100* 27.3 (Fall 2009): 35–8.

Pigliucci, Massimo and Gerd B. Müller. "Elements of an Extended Evolutionary Synthesis." In Massimo Pigliucci and Gerd B. Müller, eds. *Evolution: The Extended Synthesis*. Cambridge, MA: Massachusetts Institute of Technology Press, 2010: 3–17.

Plamper, Jan. *The History of Emotions: An Introduction.* Tribe, Keith, trans. Oxford, UK: Oxford University Press, 2015.

Probyn, Elspeth. "A-ffect: Let Her RIP." *Media/Culture Journal* 8.6 (December 2005). http://journal.media-culture.org.au/0512/13-probyn.php Accessed October 13, 2018.

Reddy, William M. *The Navigation of Feeling: A Framework for the History of Emotions.* Cambridge, UK: Cambridge University Press, 2004.

Schaefer, Donovan O. "Beautiful Facts: Science, Secularism, and Affect." In John Corrigan, ed. *Feeling Religion.* Durham, NC: Duke University Press, 2017: 69–2.

Schaefer, Donovan O. *Religious Affects: Animality, Evolution, and Power.* Durham, NC: Duke University Press, 2015.

Scheer, Monique. "Are Emotions a Kind of Practice (And Is that What Makes Them Have a History)? A Bourdieuian Approach to Understanding Emotion." *History and Theory* 51 (May 2012): 193–220.

Sedgwick, Eve Kosofsky. *The Weather in Proust.* Jonathan Goldberg, ed. Durham, NC: Duke University Press, 2011.

Sedgwick, Eve Kosofsky. *Touching Feeling: Affect, Pedagogy, Performativity.* Durham, NC: Duke University Press, 2003.

Sedgwick, Eve Kosofsky. *Tendencies.* Durham, NC: Duke University Press, 1993.

Sedgwick, Eve Kosofsky. *Epistemology of the Closet.* Berkeley, CA: University of California Press, 1990.

Seigworth, Gregory J. "Little Affect: Hallward's Deleuze." *Culture Machine.* 2007. Available at www.culturemachine.net/index.php/cm/article/view/166/147 Accessed October 13, 2018.

Shadid, Anthony. "Egyptians Wonder What's Next." *The New York Times.* January 29, 2011. Online edition. Available at: www.nytimes.com/2011/01/30/world/middleeast/30voices.html?pagewanted=all Accessed October 13, 2018.

Spinoza, Baruch. *Ethics.* Curley, Edwin, trans. New York, NY: Penguin Books, 1996.

Stewart, Kathleen. *Ordinary Affects.* Durham, NC: Duke University Press, 2007.

Sullivan, Marek. *Secular Assemblages: Affect, Orientalism, and Power in the French Enlightenment.* Unpublished doctoral dissertation, University of Oxford, 2018.

Thrush, Glenn. "What Chuck Todd Gets about Trump." *Politico.* December 30, 2016. Available at www.politico.com/story/2016/12/chuck-todd-donald-trump-off-message-podcast-233066 Accessed October 13, 2018.

Tilley, Christopher. *A Phenomenology of Landscape: Places, Paths and Monuments*. Oxford, UK: Berg, 1994.

Tomkins, Silvan S. *Affect Imagery Consciousness: The Complete Edition*. Bertram P. Karon, ed. New York, NY: Springer Publishing Company, 2008.

Tomkins, Silvan S. *Shame and Its Sisters: A Silvan Tomkins Reader*. Eve Kosofsky Sedgwick and Adam Frank, eds. Durham, NC: Duke University Press, 1995.

Tomkins, Silvan S. "The Quest for Primary Motives: Biography and Autobiography of an Idea." *Journal of Personality and Social Psychology* 41.2 (1981): 306–29.

Tomkins, Silvan S. "Script Theory: Differential Magnification of Affects." *Nebraska Symposium on Motivation* 26 (1978): 201–36.

von Uexküll, Jakob. "A Stroll through the Worlds of Animals and Men: A Picture Book of Invisible Worlds." In Claire H. Schiller, ed. *Instinctive Behavior: The Development of a Modern Concept*. New York, NY: International Universities Press, 1957: 5–80.

Wagner, Günter P. and Jeremy Draghi. "Evolution of Evolvability." In Massimo Pigliucci and Gerd B. Müller, eds. *Evolution: The Extended Synthesis*. Cambridge, MA: Massachusetts Institute of Technology Press, 2010: 379–99.

Wallace, David Foster. *Infinite Jest*. Boston, MA: Little, Brown and Company, 1996.

Weil, Kari. *Thinking Animals: Why Animal Studies Now?* New York, NY: Columbia University Press, 2012.

Wiegman, Robyn. "The Times We're in: Queer Feminist Criticism and the Reparative 'Turn.'" *Feminist Theory* 15.1 (2014): 4–25.

Wilson, Elizabeth A. *Gut Feminism*. Durham, NC: Duke University Press, 2015.

Wilson, Elizabeth A. "Organic Empathy: Feminism, Psychopharmaceuticals, and the Embodiment of Depression." In Stacy Alaimo and Susan Hekman, eds. *Material Feminisms*. Bloomington and Indianapolis, IN: Indiana University Press, 2008: 373–99.

Acknowledgments

Versions of this project have been presented in a number of venues. This project was first prompted by a generous invitation from Catherine Keller, Stephen Moore, and Karen Bray to speak at the Drew Transdisciplinary Theological Colloquium on "Affectivity and Divinity" in 2016, where the project benefited tremendously from conversation with Eugenie Brinkema, Ann Cvetkovich, Robert Davis, Amy Hollywood, Anne Joh, Jenny Knust, Jennifer Koosed, Joseph Marchal, Mary-Jane Rubenstein, Erin Runions, Rob Seesengood, Greg Seigworth, Jenna Supp-Montgomerie, and Thandeka. Another milestone was a discussion of this research at the Governing by Affect conference at the Freie Universität Berlin in June of 2017, during my time as a scholar in residence with the Affective Societies collaborative research center. I thank the conference organizers, Jan Slaby and Rainer Mühlhoff for the invitation and their thoughtful and sustained engagement with the project, the audience members for a lively discussion, and Christian von Scheve and Yasemin Ural for the invitation to take up the residency. Other facets of the project have been presented at Syracuse University and the University of the South in spring 2016 and the Society for European Philosophy conference at Regents University, London, in summer 2016. My sincerest gratitude goes to M. Gail Hamner, Sid Brown, and Tam Parker for invitations to speak on those occasions and to their students and colleagues for their comments and criticisms. I'm also grateful to Carolyn Pedwell for sharing her in-press book review of *The Ascent of Affect*, to an anonymous reviewer for a thorough and thoughtful report on the manuscript, which helped me to identify a number of cracks and flaws, and to the series editor Jan Plamper for his support of this project. Additional thanks go to Robert Spicer for calling my attention to the interview mentioned in the introduction.

Cambridge Elements ≡

Histories of Emotions and the Senses

Jan Plamper

Goldsmiths, University of London

Jan Plamper is Professor of History at Goldsmiths, University of London, where he teaches an MA seminar on the history of emotions. His publications include *The History of Emotions: An Introduction* (2015), a multidisciplinary volume on fear with contributions from neuroscience to horror film to the 1929 stock market crash, and articles on the sensory history of the Russian Revolution and the history of soldiers' fears in World War I. He has also authored *The Stalin Cult: A Study in the Alchemy of Power* (2012) and, in German, *The New We. Why Migration Is No Problem: A Different History of the Germans* (2019).

About the Series

Born of the emotional and sensory "turns," *Elements in Histories of Emotions and the Senses* move one of the fastest-growing interdisciplinary fields forward. The series is aimed at scholars across the humanities, social sciences, and life sciences, embracing insights from a diverse range of disciplines, from neuroscience to art history and economics. Chronologically and regionally broad, encompassing global, transnational, and deep history, it concerns such topics as affect theory, intersensoriality, embodiment, human-animal relations, and distributed cognition.

Cambridge Elements ≡

Histories of Emotions and the Senses

Elements in the Series

The Evolution of Affect Theory: The Humanities, the Sciences, and the Study of Power
Donovan O. Schaefer

A full series listing is available at: www.cambridge.org/EHES